March of America Facsimile Series

Number 44

Journals of
Major Robert Rogers

Robert Rogers

Journals of
Major Robert Rogers

by Robert Rogers

ANN ARBOR

UNIVERSITY MICROFILMS, INC.

A Subsidiary of Xerox Corporation

Foreword

The *Journals Of Major Robert Rogers*, published in London in 1765, describe the war experiences of perhaps the best known and most colorful colonial ranger to fight for England in the French and Indian War. In Roger's *Journals*, Englishmen, and some American colonials too, discovered a picture of frontier warfare which was probably unfamiliar to most of them. They absorbed from the *Journals* impressions of the country in the interior and of the Indians who inhabited it. Above all, they learned how determined were men like Rogers to exclude rival French power from North America.

The journal which Rogers began in September, 1755, closed with a final entry in February, 1761. During that time the author saw varied military service as a captain and later as a major in the colonial rangers. He participated in many of the most important campaigns against the French in North America, in a war which was the American counterpart of the Seven Years' War in Europe. Rogers joined in the operations at Halifax in 1757, at Ticonderoga in 1758, at Crown Point in 1759, and participated in the final campaign against the French at Montreal in 1760. After the French defeat, he set out later in the year to receive in surrender French garrisons at Detroit and at other distant posts. During the war, he had led small scouting and raiding parties deep inside enemy territory. Upon his knowledge of the country and upon his familiarity with the habits of his French and Indian enemies depended the success of his missions and the survival of his men.

Rogers felt an intense bitterness against the French. He believed that "every brave man ought to do his utmost to humble that haughty nation [France], or reduce their bounds of conquest in this country to a narrow limit." He had numerous examples to illustrate "the unheard-of-cruelties committed by the French, and the Indians, by their instigation." He claimed that the French paid their Indian allies 60 *livres* for every English scalp. He told of coming upon one Indian encampment in which "about 600 scalps, mostly English" hung from poles over the doors. However, as Rogers admitted, the English retaliated with great severity. Though Rogers had orders not to harm women or children, he was directed to take revenge upon the enemy in other ways. He was "to distress the French and their allies, by sacking, burning, and destroying their houses, barns, barracks, canoes, battoes, &c. and by killing their cattle of every kind." Rogers exulted over the defeat of France but, significantly, he felt one regret. It was a pity, he thought, that England had not also brought Louisiana into its possession, for "we should have been possessed of perhaps the most valuable territory upon the face of the globe."

Publication of Roger's *Journals* caused him to be lionized by the English press. His later activities, particularly his equivocal behavior during the American Revolution, lost him the respect of persons on both sides. Additional information about Rogers and his *Journals* can be found in Victor H. Paltsits, "Journal of Robert Rogers The Ranger on His Expedition for Receiving the Capitulation of Western French Posts," *Bulletin of the New York Public Library* (April, 1933), pp. 261-276, and in the *Dictionary of American Biography*.

✺❂✺✺❨❩✺❂✺✺❨❩✺❂✺✺❨❩✺❂✺✺❨❩✺❂✺✺❨❩✺❂✺✺❨❩✺❂✺✺❨❩✺❂✺✺

JOURNALS

O F

Major ROBERT ROGERS.

✺❂✺✺❨❩✺❂✺✺❨❩✺❂✺✺❨❩✺❂✺✺❨❩✺❂✺✺❨❩✺❂✺✺❨❩✺❂✺✺❨❩✺❂✺✺

L. SUPERIOR

Country of
Nipifsing

Peré R.

L. de

Sault St. Marie

Nipifsi.
Lake

P

Machillimakinac Ft.

Sault St. Antoine

R. St. Croix

les
Reners

R. Ouiscousing

Mascontins
Ilinois

MICHIGAM L.

L. HURON

Mission St. Ignace

le Detroit

Miamis

R. St. Joseph

St. Clair

Cou
of
th
Huro

LAKE ER

R. Mi[ifsipi

Misouri R.

R. des Osages

R. des Ilinois

R. du Teakiki

le Rocher

L. Frontenoui

Tamarois

Cascaquias

les Paniafsa

L O U

les Mentous

Arkansas R.

North or
Akancas R.

S I A

les Enie

R. Ouabache

l'Oyo ou la Belle R

R. des Chouanons

R. des Charokees ou Casquinambau

Tchicachas

Cheraquis

I

R. a Margot

Akanfas

N A

Tchactas

Ynsous

Natches

Tonicas

Natchitoches

New Orleans

Chilimachas

Mouths of the
Mississipi

Tombechi

la Mobile

Taensas

Joseph

Apalaches

Ici étoie

Georgia

F L O R I D A

A MAP of the
FRENCH
SETTLEMENTS
IN
NORTH AMERICA
By Thos. Kitchin Geogr.

English Miles
60 120 180

Longit. W. from London

JOURNALS

O F

Major ROBERT ROGERS:

CONTAINING

An Account of the feveral Excurfions he made
under the Generals who commanded upon
the Continent of NORTH AMERICA, during
the late War.

From which may by collected

The moft material Circumftances of every Campaign upon that Continent, from the Commence-
ment to the Conclufion of the War.

LONDON:

Printed for the AUTHOR,
And fold by J. MILLAN, Bookfeller, near Whitehall.
M DCC LXV.

INTRODUCTION.

IT would be offering an affront to the public, fhould I pretend to have no private views in publifhing the following JOURNALS; but they will excufe me if I leave them to conjecture what my particular views are, and claim the merit of impartially relating matters of fact, without difguife or equivocation. Moft of thofe which relate to myfelf can at prefent be attefted by living witneffes.

And fhould the troubles in America be renewed, and the favages repeat thofe fcenes of barbarity they fo often have acted on the Britifh fubjects, which there is great reafon to believe will happen, I flatter myfelf, that fuch as are immediately concerned may reap fome advantage from thefe pages.

Should any one take offence at what they may here meet with, before they venture upon exhibiting a charge, they are defired, in favour to themfelves, to confider, that I am in a fituation where they cannot attack me to their own advantage; that it is the foldier, not the fcholar, that writes; and that many things here were wrote, not with filence and leifure, but in defarts, on rocks and mountains, amidft

the

the hurries, diforders, and noife of war, and under that depreffion of fpirits, which is the natural confequence of exhaufting fatigue. This was my fituation when the following journals or accounts were tranfmitted to the generals and commanders I acted under, which I am not now at liberty to correct, except infome very grofs and palpable errors.

It would perhaps gratify the curious to have a particular account of my life, preceding the the war; but tho' I could eafily indulge them herein, without any difhonour to myfelf, yet I beg they will be content with my relating only fuch circumftances and occurrences as led me to a knowledge of many parts of the country, and tended in fome meafure to qualify me for the fervice I have fince been employed in. Such, in particular, was the fituation of the place in which I received my early education, a frontier town in the province of New Hampfhire, where I could hardly avoid obtaining fome knowledge of the manners, cuftoms, and language of the Indians, as many of them refided in the neighbourhood, and daily converfed and dealt with the Englifh.

Between the years 1743 and 1755 my manner of life was fuch as led me to a general acquaintance both with the Britifh and French fettlements in North America, and efpecially with

with the uncultivated defart, the mountains, valleys, rivers, lakes, and feveral paffes that lay between and contiguous to the faid fettlements. Nor did I content myfelf with the accounts I received from Indians, or the information of hunters, but travelled over large tracts of the country myfelf, which tended not more to gratify my curiofity, than to inure me to hardfhips, and, without vanity I may fay, to qualify me for the very fervice I have fince been employed in.

About this time the proceedings of the French in America were fuch as excited the jealoufy of the Englifh, efpecially in New York and New England ; and as Crown Point was the place from which, for many years, the Indians in the French intereft had been fitted out againft our fettlements on the frontiers, a defign was formed in the beginning of 1755 to difpoffefs them of that poft ; purfuant to which troops were levied in the feveral provinces of New England, New York, and New Jerfey. The general rendezvous was appointed at Albany in the province of New York, and the troops put under the command of Major General (fince Sir William) Johnfon. I had the honour of commanding a company in the troops furnifhed by the province of New Hampfhire, with which I made feveral

ex.

excurfions, purfuant to fpecial orders from the governor of that province, on the northern and weftern frontiers, with a view to deter the French and their Indians from making inroads upon us that way. In this manner I was employed till the month of July, when I received orders to repair to Albany, at which place I tarried till Auguft 26th, and was then ordered with 100 men to efcort the provifion-waggons from thence to the Carrying-Place, then fo called, fince Fort Edward. Here I waited upon the General, to whom I was recommended as a perfon well acquainted with the haunts and paffes of the enemy, and the Indian method of fighting, and was by him difpatched with fmall parties on feveral tours towards the French pofts, and was on one of thefe up Hudfon's River on the 8th of September, when Baron Diefkau was made prifoner, and the French and Indians under his command defeated, at the fouth-end of Lake George.

The 24th of September I received orders from the General to proceed with four men to Crown Point, and, if practicable, to bring a prifoner from thence; and with an account of the manner in which I executed thefe orders I fhall begin my JOURNALS.

A

A

JOURNAL, &c.

September 24, 1755.

PURSUANT to orders of this date from Major-General Johnfon, Commander in Chief of the Provincial Forces, raifed for the reduction of Crown Point, I embarked with four men upon Lake George, to reconnoitre the ftrength of the enemy, and proceeding down the lake twenty-five miles, I landed on the weft-fide, leaving two men in charge of the boat, while I marched with the other two till the 29th, when I had a fair view of the fort at Crown Point, and difcovered a large body of Indians round the fort, and, from their repeated irregular firing, fuppofed they

B   were

were shooting at marks, (a diversion much in use among the savages). At night I crept through the enemy's guards into a small village lying south of the fort, and passed their centries to an eminence south-west of it, from whence I discovered they were building a battery, and had already thrown up an entrenchment on that side of the fort. The next day, from an eminence at a small distance from the former, I discovered an encampment, which extended from the fort south-east to a wind-mill, at about thirty yards distance; as near as I could judge, their number amounted to about 500 men: but finding no opportunity to procure a captive, and that our small party was discovered, I judged it proper to begin a retreat homeward the 1st of October. I took my route within two miles of Ticonderoga, from whence I observed a large smoak to arise, and heard the explosion of a number of small arms; but our provisions being expended, we could not tarry to ascertain the number of the enemy there. On the 2d we arrived at the place where we left our boat in the charge of two men, but to our great mortification found they were gone, and no provisions left. This circumstance hastened us to the encampment with all possible speed, where we arrived the

4th,

4th, not a little fatigued and diſtreſſed with hunger and cold.

October 7, 1755. I received orders of this date from General Johnſon, to embark with five men under my command to reconnoitre the French troops at Ticonderoga. Accordingly I proceeded at night to a point of land on the weſt-ſide of the lake, where we landed, hid our canoe, and left two men in charge of it. The next day, with the other three, I marched to the point at Ticonderoga, where we arrived about noon. I here obſerved a body of men, which I judged to be about 2000 in number, who had thrown up an entrenchment, and prepared large quantities of hewn timber in the adjacent woods. We remained here the ſecond night, and next morning ſaw them lay the foundation of a fort, on the point which commands the paſs from Lake George to Lake Champlain, and the entrance of South Bay, or Wood Creek. Having made what diſcoveries we could, we began our return, in which we found that the enemy had a large advanced guard at the north-end of Lake George, where the river iſſues out of it into Lake Champlain. While we were viewing theſe, I obſerved a bark-canoe, with nine Indians and a Frenchman in it, going up the lake. We kept ſight

of

of them till they paffed the point of land, where our canoe and men were left, where, when we arrived, we had information from our people that the above Indians and Frenchman had landed on an ifland fix miles to the fouth of us, near the middle of the lake. In a fhort time after, we faw them put off from the ifland, and fteer directly towards us; upon which we put ourfelves in readinefs to receive them in the beft manner we could, and gave them a falute at about 100 yards diftance, which reduced their number to four. We then took boat and purfued them down the lake, till they were relieved by two canoes, which obliged us to retreat towards our encampment at Lake George, where we arrived the 10th of October.

October 15, 1755. Agreeable to orders of this date from General Johnfon, I embarked with forty men in five boats. Our defign was to difcover the ftrength of the enemy's advanced guard, and, if poffible, to decoy the whole, or part of them, into an ambufh; but tho' we were indefatigable in our endeavours for feveral days, yet all our attempts of this kind proved abortive; and, as an account of our feveral movements during this fcout would little gratify the reader, I fhall omit giving a particular detail of them. We returned fafe

to

to our encampment at Lake George on the
19th.

October 21, 1755. I had orders from
General Johnson of this date, to embark for
Crown Point, with a party of four men, in
quest of a prisoner. At night we landed on
the west-side of Lake George, twenty-five
miles from the English camp. The remainder of the way we marched by land, and the
26th came in sight of the fort. In the evening we approached nearer, and next morning
found ourselves within about 300 yards of it.
My men lay concealed in a thicket of willows,
while I crept something nearer, to a large pine-
log, where I concealed myself by holding
bushes in my hand. Soon after sun-rise the
soldiers issued out in such numbers, that my
men and I could not possibly join each other
without a discovery. About 10 o'clock a single
man marched out directly towards our ambush.
When I perceived him within ten yards of me,
I sprung over the log, and met him, and offered him quarters, which he refused, and
made a pass at me with a dirk, which I avoid-
ed, and presented my fusee to his breast; but
notwithstanding, he still pushed on with resolution, and obliged me to dispatch him. This
gave an alarm to the enemy, and made it necessary

cessary for us to hasten to the mountain. I arrived safe at our camp the 30th, with all my party.

November 4, 1755. Agreeable to orders from General Johnson this day, I embarked for the enemy's advanced guard before mentioned, with a party of thirty men, in four battoes, mounted with two wall-pieces each. The next morning, a little before day-light, we arrived within half a mile of them, where we landed, and concealed our boats; I then sent out four men as spies, who returned the next evening, and informed me, that the enemy had no works round them, but lay entirely open to an assault; which advice I dispatched immediately to the General, desiring a sufficient force to attack them, which, notwithstanding the General's earnestness and activity in the affair, did not arrive till we were obliged to retreat. On our return, however, we were met by a reinforcement, sent by the General, whereupon I returned again towards the enemy, and the next evening sent two men to see if the enemy's centries were alert, who approached so near as to be discovered and fired at by them, and were so closely pursued in their retreat, that unhappily our whole party was discovered. The first notice I had of this

this being the cafe, was from two canoes with
thirty men in them, which I concluded came
out with another party by land, in order to
force us between two fires; to prevent which,
I, with Lieutenant Mc Curdy, and fourteen men,
embarked in two boats, leaving the remainder
of the party on fhore, under the command of
Captain Putnam.——In order to decoy the enemy within the reach of our wall-pieces, we
fteered as if we intended to pafs by them, which
lucikly anfwered our expectations; for they
boldly headed us till within about an hundred
yards, when we difcharged the before mentioned pieces, which killed feveral of them,
and put the reft to flight, in which we drove
them fo near where our land-party lay, that
they were again galled by them; feveral of
the enemy were tumbled into the water, and
their canoes rendered very leaky. At this time
I difcovered their party by land, and gave our
people notice of it, who thereupon embarked
likewife, without receiving any confiderable
injury from the enemy's fire, notwithftanding
it was for fome time very brifk upon them.
We warmly purfued the enemy, and again
got an opportunity to difcharge our wall-pieces
upon them, which confufed them much, and
obliged them to difperfe.——We purfued them
down

down the lake to their landing, where they were received and covered by 100 men, upon whom we again difcharged our wall-pieces, and obliged them to retire; but finding their number vaftly fuperior to our's, we judged it moft prudent to return to our encampment at Lake George, where we fafely arrived on the 8th of November.

Nov. 10, 1755. Purfuant to orders I received this day from Gen. Johnfon, in order to difcover the enemy's ftrength and fituation at Ticonderoga, I proceeded on the fcout with a party of ten men, on the 12th inftant, and on the 14th arrived within view of the fort at that place, and found they had erected three new barracks and four ftore-houfes in the fort, between which and the water they had eighty battoes hauled upon the beach, and about fifty tents near the fort; they appeared to be very bufy at work. Having by thefe difcoveries anfwered the defign of our march, we returned, and arrived at our encampment the 19th of November.

December 19, 1755. Having had a month's repofe, I proceeded, agreeable to orders from General Johnfon, with two men, once more to reconnoitre the French at Ticonderoga. In our way we difcovered a fire upon an ifland

ad-

adjacent to the route we took, which, as we suppofed, had been kindled by fome of the ene-my who were there. This obliged us to lie by and act like fifhermen, the better to deceive them, till night came on, when we proceeded and retired to the weft-fide of the lake, fifteen miles north of our fort. Here concealing our boat, the 20th we purfued our march by land, and on the 21ft, at noon, were in fight of the French fort, where we found their people ftill deeply engaged at work, and difcovered four pieces of cannon mounted on the fouth-eaft baftion, two at the north-weft towards the woods, and two on the fouth. By what I judged, the number of their troops were about 500. I made feveral attempts to take a pri-foner, by way-laying their paths; but they al-ways paffed in numbers vaftly fuperior to mine, and thereby difappointed me. We approach-ed very near their fort by night, and were driven by the cold which now was very fe-vere) to take fhelter in one of their evacuated huts; before day, there was a fall of fnow, which obliged us with all poffible fpeed to march homeward, left the enemy fhould per-ceive our tracks and purfue us.

We found our boat in fafety, and had the good fortune (after being almoft exhaufted

C   with

with hunger, cold, and fatigue) to kill two
deer, with which being refreshed, on the
24th we returned to Fort William Henry
(a fortress erected in this year's campaign) at
the south-end of Lake George. About this
time General Johnson retired to Albany, to
which place commissioners were sent from the
several governments whose troops had been
under his command (New Hampshire only
excepted). These commissioners were em-
powered by their respective constituents, with
the assent of a council of war, to garrison Fort
William Henry and Fort Edward, for that
winter, with part of the troops that had served
the preceding year. Accordingly a regiment
was formed, to which Boston government
furnished a Colonel—Connecticut a Lieute-
nant-Colonel—and New York a Major: after which it was adjudged, both by Gen. Johnson and these Commissioners, that it would be
of great use to leave one company of woods-
men or rangers under my command, to make
excursions towards the enemy's forts during
the winter; I accordingly remained, and did
duty the whole winter, until called upon by
General Shirley.

January 14, 1756. I this day marched
with a party of seventeen men, to reconnoitre
the

the French forts; we proceeded down the lake, on the ice, upon fkaits, and halted for refrefhment near the fall out of Lake George into Lake Champlain.—At night we renewed our march, and, by day-break on the 16th, formed an ambufh on a point of land on the eaft-fhore of Lake Champlain, within gun-fhot of the path in which the enemy paffed from one fort to the other. About fun-rife, two fledges laden with frefh beef were prefented to our view, we intercepted the drivers, de-ftroyed their loading, and afterwards re-turned to Fort William Henry, where I ar-rived with my prifoners and party in good health the 17th.

January 26, 1756. Purfuant to orders of this date, from Colonel Glafier, I marched from Lake George with a party of fifty men, with a defign to difcover the ftrength and works of the enemy at Crown Point.

On the 2d of February, we arrived within a mile of that fortrefs, where we climbed a very fteep mountain, from which we had a clear and full profpect of the fort, and an op-portunity of taking a plan of the enemy's works there. In the evening we retired to a fmall village, half a mile from the fort, and

formed

formed an ambufcade on each fide of the road leading from the fort to the village. Next morning a Frenchman fell into our hands; foon after we difcovered two more, but they unluckily got fight of us before they were in our power, and haftily retired to the fort. Finding ourfelves difcovered by the enemy by this accident, we employed ourfelves while we dared ftay in fetting fire to the houfes and barns of the village, with which were con-fumed large quantities of wheat, and other grain; we alfo killed about fifty cattle, and then retired, leaving the whole village in flames, and arrived fafe at our fort, with our prifoner, the 6th of February.

February 29, 1756. Agreeable to orders from Colonel Glafier, I this day marched with a party of fifty-fix men down the weft-fide of Lake George. We continued our route north-ward till the 5th of March, and then fteered eaft to Lake Champlain, about fix miles north of Crown Point, where, by the in-telligence we had from the Indians, we ex-pected to find fome inhabited villages.—We then attempted to crofs the lake, but found the ice too weak. The 17th we returned and marched round the bay to the weft of Crown Point, and at night got into the cleared
land

land among their houfes and barns; here we
formed an ambufh, expecting their labourers
out to tend their cattle, and clean their grain,
of which there were feveral barns full; we
continued there that night, and next day till
dark, when, difcovering none of the enemy,
we fet fire to the houfes and barns, and
marched off. In our return I took a frefh
view of Ticonderoga, and reconnoitered the
ground between that fort and the advanced
guard on Lake George, approaching fo near as
to fee their centries on the ramparts, and obtained all the knowledge of their works,
ftrength, and fituation, that I defired.

The 14th of March, we returned fafe to
Fort William Henry.

The next day, after my return from this
fcout, I received a letter, dated February 24,
1756, from Mr. William Alexander of New-
York, who was fecretary to Mr. Shirley,
Commander in chief of the troops at Ofwego
the preceding year, and who now, upon the
deceafe of General Braddock, fucceeded to
the chief command of all his Majefty's forces
in North America, and was now at Bofton,
preparing for the enfuing campaign, being
previoufly recommended to this gentleman by
Gene-

General Johnfon. I was defired by the above-mentioned letter to wait on him at Bofton; of which I informed the commanding officer at the fort, and, with his approbation, I fet out on the 17th of March, leaving the command of my company to Mr. Noah Johnfon, my Enfign; my brother Richard Rogers, who was my Lieutenant, being fent to Bofton by the commanding officer, on fome difpatches previous to this.

On the 23d, I waited on the General, and met with a very friendly reception; he foon intimated his defign of giving me the command of an independent company of rangers, and the very next morning I received the commiffion, with a fet of inftructions.

According to the General's orders, my company was to confift of fixty privates, at 3 s. New York currency *per* day, three ferjeants at 4 s. an Enfign at 5 s. a Lieutenant at 7 s. and my own pay was fixed at 10 s. *per* day. Ten Spanifh dollars were allowed to each man towards providing cloaths, arms, and blankets. My orders were, to raife this company as quick as poffible, to inlift none but fuch as were ufed to travelling and hunting, and in whofe courage and fidelity I could confide:
they

they were, moreover, to be subject to military discipline, and the articles of war.

Our rendezvous was appointed at Albany, from thence to proceed in four whale-boats to Lake George, and, " from time to time, " to use my best endeavours to distress the " French and their allies, by sacking, burning, " and destroying their houses, barns, barracks, " canoes, battoes, &c. and by killing their cattle " of every kind; and at all times to endeavour " to way-lay, attack, and destroy their convoys " of provisions by land and water, in any part " of the country, where I could find them."

With these instructions, I received letters to the commanding officers, at Fort William-Henry and Fort Edward, directing them to forward the service, with which I was now particularly charged.

When my company was completed, a part marched under the command of Lieutenant Rogers to Albany; with the remainder, I was ordered to march through the woods to No. 4, then a frontier town greatly exposed to the enemy; where,

April 28, 1756, I received orders to march from thence to Crown Point, in pursuance of which we travelled through deserts and mountains. The second day of our march, my

second

second Lieutenant, Mr. John Stark, was taken fick, and obliged to return, with whom I fent fix men to guard him to Fort Edward.

We continued our march till the 5th of May, when I arrived with nine men at Lake Champlain, four miles fouth of Crown Point. Here we concealed our packs, and marched up to a village on the eaft-fide, about two miles diftant from Crown Point, but found no inhabitant there. We lay in wait the whole day following, oppofite to Crown Point, expecting fome party to crofs the lake ; but nothing appeared except about four or five hundred men in canoes and battoes, coming up the lake from St. John's to Crown Point. We kept our ftations till next day, ten o'clock A. M. to obferve the motions of the enemy, but finding no opportunity to trapan any of them, we killed twenty three head of cattle, the tongues of which was a very great refrefhment to us on our journey. We at this time difcovered eleven canoes manned with a confiderable number of French and Indians croffing the lake directly towards us, upon which we retired ; and the better to efcape our purfuers we difperfed, each man taking a different route. We afterwards affembled at the place where we concealed our packs, and on a raft croffed over to the weft-
fide

fide of the lake. In our way we had a view of the French and Indians, encamped at the old Indian carrying-place, near Ticonderoga, and the 11th of May arrived fafe at Fort William-Henry. Mr. Stark, with his party, arrived at Fort Edward three days before. In their way they difcovered a fcouting party of three or four hundred Indians. Lieutenant Rogers with his party had arrived fome days before this, and was at this time out upon a fcout.

May 20, 1756. Agreeable to orders from the General, I fet out with a party of eleven men to reconnoitre the French advanced guards. The next day, from the top of a mountain, we had a view of them, and judged their number to be about 300 ; they were bu-fy in fortifying themfelves with palifadoes. From the other fide of the mountain we had a profpect of Ticonderoga fort, and, from the ground their encampment took up, I judged it to confift of about 1000 men. This night we lodged on the mountain, and next morning marched to the Indian carrying-path, that leads from Lake George to Lake Champlain, and formed an ambufcade between the French guards and Ticonderoga fort. About fix o'clock 118 Frenchmen paffed by without

D   dif-

discovering us; in a few minutes after, twenty-two more came the same road, upon whom we fired, killed six, and took one a prisoner; but the large party returning, obliged us to retire in haste, and we arrived safe, with our prisoner, at Fort William Henry the 23d.

The prisoner we had taken reported, "that a party of 220 French and Indians were preparing to invest the out-parties at Fort Edward," which occasioned my marching the next morning with a party of 78 men, to join a detachment of Col. Bayley's regiment, to scour the woods as far as South Bay, if possible to intercept the enemy; but we could not discover them.

June 13, 1756. Agreeable to orders this evening, I embarked with a party of 26 men in battoes upon Lake George, to revisit the French advanced guard; excessive thunder and lightening obliged us to land at about ten miles distance from our fort, where we spent the night. The next morning, about sun-rise, we heard the explosion of upwards of twenty small arms, on the opposite side of the lake, which we supposed to be a party of French and Indians, cleaning their guns after the rain. In the evening we embarked again, and

and early in the morning of the 16th drew
up our battoes about four miles diftant from
the advanced guard, and afterwards lay in
ambufh by a path leading from thence to a
mountain, in order to furprize the enemy,
who went there daily in parties, to take a
view of the lake; but finding they were not
at that place, we marched to the fpot where
the enemy had pofted their advanced guard,
but they had retired and demolifhed all their
works there; we then continued our march
towards Ticonderoga, near which place we
afcended an eminence, and had a clear view
of their works. I judged that their garrifon and encampment confifted of about
3000 men : We then fet out on our return, and arrived at Fort William-Henry
the 18th inftant, except one man, who
ftrayed from us, and who did not get in
till the 23d, then almoft famifhed for want
of fuftenance.

About this time the General augmented my
company to feventy men, and fent me fix light
whale-boats from Albany, with orders to
proceed immediately to Lake Champlain, to
cut off, if poffible, the provifions and flying
parties of the enemy. Accordingly,

June

June 28, 1756, I embarked with fifty men in five whale-boats, and proceeded to an island in Lake George. The next day, at about five miles diftance from this ifland, we landed our boats, and carried them about fix miles over a mountain, to South Bay, where we arrived the 3d of July. The following evening we embarked again, and went down the bay to within fix miles of the French fort, where we concealed our boats till the evening. We then embarked again, and paffed by Ticonderoga undifcovered, tho' we were fo near the enemy as to hear their centry's watchword. We judged from the number of their fires, that they had a body of about 2000 men, and the lake in this place to be near 400 yards wide. About five miles further down, we again concealed our boats, and lay by all day. We faw feveral battoes going and coming upon the lake. At night we put off again, with a defign to pafs by Crown Point, but afterwards judged it imprudent by reafon of the clearnefs of the night, fo lay concealed again the next day, when near a hundred boats paffed by us, feven of which came very near the point where we were, and would have landed there; but the officer infifted, in our hearing, upon going about 150 yards further, where they landed, and dined

dined in our view. About nine o'clock at night we re-imbarked, and paffed the fort at Crown Point, and again concealed our boats at about 10 miles diftance from it. This day, being July 7th, 30 boats, and a fchooner of about 30 or 40 tons, paffed by us towards Canada. We fet out again in the evening, and landed about fifteen miles further down, from which place I fent a party for further difcovery, who brought intelligence of a fchooner at anchor, about a mile from us; we immediately lightened our boats, and prepared to board her; but were prevented by two lighters coming up the lake, who, we found, intended to land where we were pofted; thefe we fired upon, then hailed them, and offered them quarters, if they would come afhore; but they haftily pufhed towards the oppofite fhore, where we purfued and intercepted them: we found their number to be twelve, three of which were killed by our fire, and two wounded, one of them in fuch a manner that he foon died. We funk and deftroyed their veffels and cargoes, which confifted chiefly of wheat and flour, wine and brandy; fome few cafks of the latter we carefully concealed. The prifoners informed us, that they were a part of 500 men,

men, the remainder of which were not far behind on their paſſage, which induced us to
haſten our return to our garriſon, where, with
our priſoners, we ſafely arrived the 15th of
July. Theſe priſoners, upon examination, reported, " That a great number of regular troops
and militia were aſſembling at Chamblee, and
deſtined for Carillon, or Ticonderoga * : that
great quantities of proviſions were tranſporting
there, and a new General ✝ with two regiments lately arrived from France : that there
was no talk of any deſign upon our forts
on this ſide ; but that a party of 300 French,
and 20 Indians, had already ſet out to intercept
our convoys of proviſions between Albany and
Lake George : that 60 livres was the reward
for an Engliſh ſcalp, and that the priſoners
were ſold in Canada for 50 crowns each : that
their proſpect of an harveſt was very encouraging, but that the ſmall-pox made great ha-
vock amongſt the inhabitants." About the
time of my ſetting out upon this ſcout, Major
General Shirley was ſuperſeded in his command

* The former is the French, the latter the Indian name,
ſignifying the meeting or confluence of three waters.
✝ The Marquis de Montcalm, who commanded in the
reduction of Oſwego this year, and of Fort William-Henry
the year following.

mand by Major General Abercrombie, who
arrived at the head-quarters in Albany on the
25th of June, and brought with him two
regiments of regular troops from England.
I therefore, upon my return, wrote to his Excellency, defiring leave to lay before him the minutes of my laft fcout, and to recommend to his
confideration an augmentation of the rangers.
The General permitted me, with my brother
Richard Rogers, to wait upon him at Albany.
In this interview we difcourfed on the fubject
of my letter, in confequence of which he immediately ordered a new company of rangers
to be raifed, and gave the command of it to my
brother *, appointed Noah Johnfon, my former Enfign, his Firft Lieutenant, Nathaniel
Abbot his Second Lieutenant, and Caleb Page
his Enfign. John Stark, formerly my Second
Lieutenant, was appointed my Firft, John
M'Curdy fucceeded to his place, and Jonathan Burbank was appointed my Enfign.

August 2, 1756. Agreeable to orders received of General Abercrombie at Albany,
the 23d of July, I embarked this day at Fort
William-Henry, on board one of the lighters
built

* He compleated his company in 28 days, and, by the
General's orders, went up Mohawke river, to ferve as
a fcouting party for the troops that way.

built there this summer, with twenty-five of
my company, in order to reconnoitre the e-
nemy at Ticonderoga and Crown Point, and
sixty men under Capt. Larnard of the provincials, who had General Winflow's * orders to
proceed with his men to the French advanced
guard ; but he not being acquainted with the
way thither, put himself under my command.
We landed this morning about fifteen miles
down Lake George, and proceeded with the
party till the 4th in the evening, and encamped
about a mile from the advanced guard. The
5th in the morning muftered the whole party,
and got to the fummit of a hill, weft of the advanced guard, where we difcovered two advanced pofts, which I then imagined was the
whole of the guard, one of them on the weft-
fide, half a mile fouthward of Lake Champlain, the other on the eaft-fide of the Lake,
oppofite the former, at the old Indian carrying-
place. We judged there were about 400 men
on the eaft, and 200 on the weft. After de-
liberating with Capt. Larnard upon the ftrength
and

---

* General Winflow commanded the provincial troops
this year, by virtue of a commiffion from the feveral provinces, who were concerned in 1755, in the fame expedition, and was now with the greateft part of the provincial
troops at Lake George.

and difpofition of the enemy, and the report of our advanced party, we concluded it unadvife-able to continue there any longer. He return-ed towards Fort William-Henry, and I went on with my own party till we came within view of Ticonderoga Fort, where, from an eminence, I difcovered the fituation, but could not afcertain the ftrength of it to my fatisfac-tion.

Auguft 6, I went down towards Crown Point, by the weft-fide of Lake Champlain, and difcovered feveral battoes paffing from that place to Ticonderoga with troops on board. We then proceeded to the place where we burnt the village, as mentioned before, and there encamped, and perceived a party fally-ing out, driving a number of horfes to feed.

The 7th we lay in ambufh by the road, with a defign to intercept fuch as might come out to drive in the cattle ; but no one appearing for that purpofe, we approached nearer, to within half a mile of the fort, where we were difcovered by two Frenchmen, before they were in our power. This accident obliged us to make a retreat, in which we killed upwards of forty cattle. We arrived at Fort William-Henry, Auguft 10.

E

A com-

A company of Stockbridge Indians was this year employed in his Majefty's fervice, commanded by Indian officers, properly commiffioned by General Shirley, before he was fuperfeded in his command. General Abercrombie was fomewhat at a lofs how to difpofe of this company, and applied to Sir William Johnfon, who advifed, that a part *, viz. thirty privates and a Lieutenant, fhould fcout and fcour the woods under my direction, which party had arrived while I was out upon my laft fcout, and Lieutenant Stark had ftrengthened their party with fome of our people, and fent them out with particular directions what route to take, the day before I arrived.

About this time his Excellency the Earl of Loudoun arrived at Albany, and had taken upon him the command of the army, to whom I applied as I had done before to Gen. Abercrombie, tranfmitting to him an account of the Indian fcout above-mentioned (who returned the 13th with two French fcalps, agreeable to their barbarous cuftom) and defiring that with them I might attempt to penetrate into Canada,

and

---

* The remainder of this Indian company, with their Captain, were fent to Saratoga, to be under the direction of Colonel Burton.

and diftrefs the inhabitants, by burning their harveft (now nearly ripe) and deftroying their cattle.

Accordingly, Auguft 16, we embarked in whale-boats in two departments, the one commanded by Lieutenant Stark, the other by myfelf.—The next morning we joined each other, at which time alfo fell in with us a party of eight Mohocks, who had marched out from Fort William Henry the day before. We then marched directly to the place where we left our whale-boats the 7th of July, proceeding about twenty-five miles northward of Crown Point fort, on the weft-fide of Lake Champlain, where we all (excepting one man who ftrayed from us and returned) arrived fafe the 24th. We embarked again in our boats, and fteered down the lake towards St. John's. The 25th we proceeded twenty miles further, and about midnight difcovered a fchooner ftanding up the lake with a fair wind towards Crown Point; they paffed us fo fwiftly that we could not poffibly board her, as we intended.

The 26th we landed, and the Mohocks left us to join another party of theirs then out on a fcout.

The

The 27th we got on a point, with a defign to intercept the enemy's battoes that might pafs up and down the lake ; but not difcovering any, and our provifions growing fhort, we returned up the lake, and landed eight miles north of the fort at Crown Point, on the eaft-fide of the lake.

The 29th in the morning we marched to a village lying eaft of the fort, and in our way took prifoners, a man, his wife, and daughter, (a girl about fourteen years of age) ; with thefe prifoners we returned, and arrived fafe at Fort William-Henry, Sept. 22, 1756.

The man-prifoner, above-mentioned, upon examination, reported, " That he was born " at Vaifac, in the province of Guienne in " France : that he had been in Canada about " fifteen years, and in the colonies fervice " about fix, and two years at Crown Point : " that there were only 300 men at Crown " Point, and thofe chiefly inhabitants of the " adjacent villages ; that there were 4000 men " at Ticonderoga or Carillon, 1500 of which " were regular troops, who had a fufficiency of " all kinds of provifions : that he never was " at Ticonderoga or at the advance guard, " but heard there were only fifteen men at " the latter : that the French had 600 Indians

" ans at Ticonderoga, and expected 600 more:
" that 1200 were arrived at Quebec for Ca-
" rillon, which laſt 1800 hundred were un-
" der the command of Monſ. Scipio de la
" Maſure: that they had a great quantity of
" cannon, mortars, ſhells, &c. at Ticondero-
" ga, but he did not know the number or
" quantity: that they expected the above re-
" inforcement in two or three days at Ticon-
" deroga, having ſent boats to Montreal to
" fetch them: that they underſtood by a let-
" ter that Oſwego had fallen into their hands,
" but the news was not confirmed: that they
" had heard we intended to inveſt Carillon,
" but did not know what movements were
" intended on their ſide ſhould we neglect it:
" that they had 150 battoes on Lake Cham-
" plain, which were kept at Carillon, thirty-
" five of which conſtantly plied between Mon-
" treal and that fortreſs: that Monſ. Mont-
" calm commanded at Frontiniac with 5000
" men, but did not know whether theſe
" troops were regulars or provincials: that a
" great number of veſſels had arrived at Ca-
" nada with proviſions and military ſtores:
" that they heard we had ſeveral ſhips in the
" river St. Lawrence: that Monſ. de Conte
" de Levi commanded at Carillon, and came
                                        " laſt

" laſt May from France ; and that, ſince the
" two laſt ſhallops or lighters (before-menti-
" oned) were taken, they had augmented the
" number of men on board the large ſchooner
" in Lake Champlain from twelve to thirty."

Upon my return to the fort, I received orders from my Lord Loudon to wait upon
Col. Burton, of the 48th regiment, for inſtructions, he being then poſted at Saratoga. By
him I was ordered to return to my company at
Fort William-Henry, and march them to the
South Bay, thence eaſt to the Wood Creek,
then to croſs it ſoutherly, oppoſite to Saratoga,
and return and make my report to him.

In this tour we apprehended four deſerters
from Otway's regiment, who were going to
the enemy, and whom I ſent back to Fort Edward, with a part of my detachment, under
the command of Lieutenant Stark, and proceeded with the remainder to compleat my
orders, after which I returned to Saratoga to
make my report.

There I met my brother Capt. Richard Rogers with his company, he being ordered back
from Mohock river, to join me with the remainder of the Stockbridge Indians ; and I marched
both companies to Fort Edward, where I was
ordered to form an encampment. A part of
the

the Indian company were fent out on the eaft-
fide of Lake Champlain to alarm the enemy at
Ticonderoga, whilft I, with a detachment of
my own, and Capt. Richard Rogers's company, was ordered on another party down
Lake George, in whale-boats, and the remainder of the companies were employed in
reconnoitering round the encampment, and
alfo ferved as flankers to the parties that
guarded provifions to Lake George. Capt. Jacob, who commanded the Indian party before-
mentioned, returned two days before me
with four French fcalps, which they took oppofite to Ticonderoga on the eaft-fide.

Sept. 7, 1756. Agreeable to orders, I this
day embarked on Lake George, with a party of
fourteen men in a whale-boat, which we
landed, and concealed the evening following,
on the eaft-fhore, about four miles fouth of
the French advance guard. Here I divided
my party, taking feven men with me, leaving
the remainder in charge of Mr. Chalmer (a
volunteer fent me by Sir John Sinclair) with
orders, upon his difcovering the enemy's boats
going up the lake, &c. to make the beft of
his way with the intelligence to Fort William-
Henry.

I was

I was the 9th current within half a mile of Ticonderoga fort, where I endeavoured to reconnoitre the enemy's works and ftrength. They were engaged in raifing the walls of the fort, and had erected a large block-houfe near the fouth-eaft corner of the fort, with ports in it for cannon. Eaft from the block-houfe was a battery, which I imagined commanded the lake. I difcovered five houfes fouth of the fort clofe to the water-fide, and 160 tents fouth-weft of the fort, and twenty-feven battoes hauled upon the beach.

Next morning, with one private, I went to view the falls betwixt Lake Champlain and Lake George (where I had heard the explofion of feveral guns the evening before, and had at that time, fent Serjeant Henry to difcover the reafon of it) leaving the remainder of my party in charge of Mr. Gibbs, another volunteer, to wait our return. Serjeant Henry followed foon after me, and reported, " that the " French were building a fmall fort at the " head of the falls on the eaft-fide of the lake; " that he alfo difcovered their guard to the " weftward, and imagined both confifted of " 500 men." I returned, after finding the French were engaged in building a faw-mill at the lower end of the falls, and found my

boats,

boats with provisions left, as I suppose, by Mr. Chalmer and his party, whom I waited for till seven o'clock next day; but he not returning, and I judging from their tracks that they were returned to Fort William-Henry, we likewise began our return, and arrived safe the 11th of September, where I found Mr. Chalmer and the party left with him, he having punctually obeyed the orders given him above. Upon my return, I communicated my observations upon the Lakes George and Champlain to my Lord Loudoun, giving him as just a description as I could of their situation.

September 24, General Abercrombie issued out orders, that three commissioned officers of the rangers, with 20 privates each, should reconnoitre the Wood Creek, South Bay, and Ticonderoga; and these were alternately sent out, so that a continual scout was kept up for a considerable time.

October 22, 1756. The greatest part of the army was now at Fort-Edward, under the command of General Abercrombie, and Lord Loudoun arriving about this time with the remainder, it was generally expected that the army would cross the lake, and endeavour to reduce the French forts, notwithstanding the season was so far advanced; but his Lordship

F   taking

taking into confideration the probability that thofe lakes would freeze (which they generally do in the month of December) in which cafe no fupplies could be had from, nor any communication kept up with Fort William-Henry; he determined to defift from this defign, and contented himfelf with keeping the field till Monf. Montcalm retired to winter-quarters, and accordingly fought all opportunities to learn his fituation and movements.

Agreeable to orders from his Lordfhip, I this day embarked in two whale-boats, with a party of twenty men, upon Lake George, with an intent to bring a prifoner from Ticonderoga. We paffed the Narrows twenty miles from our embarkation, when Capt. Shephard (who was made a captive in Auguft laft and carried to Canada) hailed our boat; I knew his voice, and took him on board with three other men, one of whom was taken with him. He reported, that he left Canada fifteen days before. I went on my courfe till the 27th, towards Carillon, and landed that night on the weft-fide of the lake, concealed our boats, and travelled by land to within a mile of the fort. I kept fpies out the day after to improve any opportunity that might offer,

offer, and the next day fent them ftill nearer, but to no good purpofe: I at length difcovered two men, centries to the piquet guard of the French army, one of which was pofted on the road that leads from the fort to the woods: I took five of my party, and marched directly down the road in the middle of the day, till we were challenged by the centry. I anfwered in French, fignifying that we were friends; the centinel was thereby deceived, till I came clofe to him, when perceiving his miftake, in great furprize he called, Qui etes vous? I anfwered, Rogers, and led him from his poft in great hafte, cutting his breeches and coat from him, that he might march with the greater eafe and expedition. With this prifoner we arrived at Fort WilliamHenry, Oct. 31, 1756. Upon examination, he reported, "That he belonged to the regi
" ment of Languedoc: that he left Breft laft
" April was a twelve-month, and had ferved
" fince at Lake Champlain, Crown Point, and
" Carillon, was laft year with General Diefkaw
" in the battle at Fort William-Henry: that
" they loft in that engagement of regulars,
" Canadians, and Indians, a great number:
" that at Carillon were at this time mounted
" thirty-fix pieces of cannon, viz. twelve

eight-

" eighteen pounders, fifteen twelve pounders,
" and nine eight pounders: that at Crown
" Point were eighteen pieces, the largeft of
" which were eighteen pounders: that Monf.
" Montcalm's forces this year at Carillon were
" 3000 regulars, and 2000 Canadians and In-
" dians: that Montcalm himfelf was drawn
" off with one battalion, and that the forces
" then in that neighbourhood confifted of five
" battalions and about 800 Canadians: that
" the Indians were all gone off, 200 of whom
" talked of returning to fpend the winter at
" Carillon: that the advanced guard on the
" weft-fide above the falls were all drawn in,
" and that that on the eaft confifted of 600
" men, who were to decamp the 1ft of Novem-
" ber: that they had a camp of five battalions,
" and fixty Canadians, about half a league from
" Carillon, and that the reft of the army were
" under the fort: that they had barracks fuf-
" ficient for 500 men, which he underftood
" were to quarter there: that they had one
" fchooner and 200 battoes on Lake Cham-
" plain, and but five or fix on Lake George:
" that Monf. the Chevalier de Levi com-
" manded in Monf. Moncalm's abfence, and
" that the Canadians were commanded by
" Meffieurs le Corn and Columbie: that when
" Mon-

" Monfieur Montcalm went off, he faid he
" had done enough for this year, and would
" take Fort William-Henry early in the fpring:
" that the French had taken four of Captain
" Rogers's whale-boats in lake Champlain :
" that when he was taken prifoner, he ima-
" gined himfelf to be about a gun-fhot and half
" from the fort, and that the French camp
" was pretty healthy."

From this time we were conftantly employed in patrolling the woods about Fort Edward till the the 19th of November 1756,
when I had his Lordfhip's orders to take another excurfion down the Lake. Captain
Abercrombie, Aid-de-camp and nephew to
General Abercrombie, did me the honour to
accompany me; but nothing material being in
our power to effect, except taking a view of
the fort and works of the enemy at Ticonderoga, we returned fafe to Fort Edward the
25th in the evening.

About this time his Lordfhip drew off the
main body of the troops from Fort Edward to
be quartered at Albany and New York.

Both armies being now retired to winter-
quarters, nothing material happened to the
end of this year. The rangers were ftationed
at the Forts William-Henry and Edward, to
which

which alfo two new companies of rangers were fent this fall, commanded by Captain Spikeman and Captain Hobbs, in one of which my brother James Rogers was appointed an Enfign.

Thefe two companies were ftationed at Fort William-Henry mine and my brother Richard's at Fort Edward.

Captain Richard Rogers had leave to go into New England for recruits to complete our two companies. He this winter waited upon the government of Bofton, to obtain pay for our fervices in the winter 1755 before-mentioned, but could obtain none, notwithftanding Lord Loudoun, who was then at Bofton, generoufly fupported and enforced our folicitations with his intereft.

January 15, 1757. Agreeable to orders from the commanding officer at Fort Edward, I this day marched with my own Lieutenant Mr. Stark, Enfign Page of Captain Richard Rogers's company, and fifty privates of faid companies, to Fort William-Henry, where we were employed in providing provifions, fnow-fhoes, &c. till the 17th, when being joined by Captain Spikeman, Lieutenant Kennedy and Enfign Brewer of his company, and fourteen of their men, together with Enfign James Rogers and

and fourteen men of Captain Hobbs's company, and Mr. Baker, a volunteer of the 44th regiment of foot, we began our march on the ice down Lake George, and at night encamped on the eaft-fide of the Firft Narrows. The next morning, finding that fome of the detachment had hurt themfelves in the march the day before, as many were difmiffed to return to the fort, as reduced our party to feventy-four men, officers included.

The 18th we marched twelve miles down the lake, and encamped on the weft-fide of it.

The 19th we marched three miles from our encampment further down the lake, and then took the land, and, upon fnow-fhoes, travelled north-weft about eight miles from our landing, and three from the lake, where we encamped.

The 20th we marched north-by-eaft the whole day, and at night encamped on the weftern-fide, oppofite to and about three miles diftant from Lake Champlain.

The 21ft we marched eaft, till we came to the lake, about mid-way between Crown Point and Ticonderoga, and immediately difcovered a fled going from the latter to the former. I ordered Lieutenant Stark, with twenty men, to head the fled, while I, with a party, marched the other way to prevent its retreating

ing back again, leaving Captain Spikeman in the center with the remainder. I soon difcovered eight or ten fleds more following down the lake, and endeavoured to give Mr. Stark intelligence of it before he fallied on the lake and difcovered himfelf to them, but could not. They all haftily returned towards Ticonderoga. We purfued them, and took feven prifoners, three fleds, and fix horfes; the remainder made their efcape. We examined the captives feparately, who reported, " That 200 Canadi-
" ans and 45 Indians were juft arrived at Ti-
" conderoga, and were to be reinforced that
" evening, or next morning, by fifty Indians
" more from Crown Point : that there were
" 600 regular troops at that fortrefs, and 350
" at Ticonderoga, where they foon expected a
" large number of troops, who in the fpring
" were to befiege our forts : that they had
" large magazines of provifions in their forts,
" and that the above-mentioned party were
" well equipped, and in a condition to march
" upon any emergency at the leaft notice, and
" were defigned foon to way-lay and diftrefs
" our convoys between the forts."

From this account of things, and knowing that thofe who efcaped would give early notice of us at Ticonderoga, I concluded it beft to return ;

turn; and ordered the party, with the utmoſt expedition, to march to the fires we had kindled the night before, and prepare for a battle, if it ſhould be offered, by drying our guns, it being a rainy day, which we effeďed; and then marched in a ſingle file, myſelf and Lieutenant Kennedy in the front, Lieutenant Stark in the rear, and Captain Spikeman in the center. Enſigns Page and Rogers were between the front and center, and Enſign Brewer between the center and rear, Serjeant Walker having the command of a rear-guard. In this manner we advanced half a mile, or thereabouts, over broken ground, when paſſing a valley of about fifteen rods breadth, the front having reached the ſummit of a hill on the weſt-ſide of it; the enemy, who had here drawn up in the form of a half-moon, with a deſign, as we ſuppoſed, to ſurround us, ſaluted us with a volley of about 200 ſhot, at the diſtance of about five yards from the neareſt, or front, and thirty from the rear of their party. This fire was about two o'clock in the afternoon, and proved fatal to Lieutenant Kennedy, and Mr. Gardner, a volunteer in my company, and wounded me and ſeveral others; myſelf, however, but ſlightly in the head. We immediately returned their fire. I then ordered my men to the oppoſite hill, where I ſuppoſed Lieutenant Stark

G   and

and Enfign Brewer had made a ftand with forty men to cover us, in cafe we were obliged to retreat. We were clofely purfued, and Capt. Spikeman, with feveral of the party, were killed, and others made prifoners. My people, however, beat them back by a brifk fire from the hill, which gave us an opportunity to afcend, and poft ourfelves to advantage. After which I ordered Lieutenant Stark and Mr. Baker in the center, with Enfign Rogers; Serjeants Walter and Phillips, with a party, being a referve, to prevent our being flanked, and watch the motions of the enemy. Soon after we had thus formed ourfelves for battle, the enemy attempted to flank us on the right, but the above referve bravely attacked them, and giving them the firft fire very brifkly, it ftopped feveral from retreating to the main body. The enemy then pufhed us clofely in the front; but having the advantage of the ground, and being fheltered by large trees, we maintained a continual fire upon them, which killed feveral, and obliged the reft to retire to their main body. They then attempted to flank us again, but were again met by our referved party, and repulfed. Mr. Baker about this time was killed. We maintained a pretty conftant fire on both fides, till the darknefs prevented our feeing each other, and about fun-fet I received a ball

thro'

thro' my hand and wrift, which difabled me from loading my gun. I however found means to keep my people from being intimidated by this accident; they gallantly kept their advantageous fituation, till the fire ceafed on both fides. The enemy, during the action, ufed many arts and ftratagems to induce us to fubmit, fometimes threatening us with feverity if we refufed, affuring us that they every moment expected a large reinforcement, which fhould cut us to pieces without mercy: at other times flattering and cajolling us, declaring it was a pity fo many brave men fhould be loft; that we fhould, upon our furrender, be treated with the greateft compaffion and kindnefs; calling me by name, they gave me the ftrongeft affurances of their efteem and friendfhip that words could do; but no one being difmayed by their menaces, or flattered by fair promifes, we told them our numbers were fufficient, and that we were determined to keep our ground as long as there were two left to ftand by each other.

After the action, in which we had a great number fo feverely wounded that they could not travel without affiftance, and our ammunition being nearly expended, and confidering that we were near to Ticonderoga, from whence the enemy might eafily make a defcent, and

over-

overpower us by numbers, I thought it expedient to take the advantage of the night to retreat, and gave orders accordingly; and the next morning arrived at Lake George, about six miles south of the French advanced guard, from whence I dispatched Lieutenant Stark with two men to Fort William-Henry, to procure conveyances for our wounded men thither; and the next morning we were met by a party of fifteen men and a sled, under the command of Lieutenant Buckley, of Hobbs's company of Rangers, at the first narrows at Lake George. Our whole party, which now consisted of only forty-eight effective, and six wounded men, arrived at Fort William-Henry the same evening, being the 23d of January 1757.

The nearest computation we could make of the number which attacked us, was, that it consisted of about 250 French and Indians; and we afterwards had an account from the enemy, that their loss in this action, of those killed, and who afterwards died of their wounds, amounted to 116 men.

Both the officers and soldiers I had the honour to command who survived the first onset, behaved with the most undaunted bravery and resolution, and seemed to vie with each other in their respective stations who should excel.

The

The following is the RETURN which was made of the Killed, Wounded, and Missing, in the above action, *viz.*

Company	Name	Killed	Missing	Wounded
Captain Rogers's Company.	Capt. Robert Rogers			Wounded
	Mr. Baker, Volunteer	Killed		
	Mr. Gardner, ditto	ditto		
	Thomas Henson —	ditto		
	Serjeant Martin —			ditto
	Thomas Burnside —			ditto
	Serjeant Henry —		Missing	
	William Morris —		ditto	
	John Morrison —		ditto	
C. Rd Rogers's do.	Joseph Stephens —	ditto		
	Benjamin Woodall		ditto	
	David Kemble —		ditto	
	Ensign Caleb Page	ditto		
	David Page —			ditto
Capt. Hobbs's ditto.	Serjeant Jn. Howard	ditto		
	Phineas Kemp —	ditto		
	John Edmonds —	ditto		
	Thomas Farmer —	ditto		
	Emanuel Lapartaquer	ditto		
Capt. Spikeman's ditto.	Capt. Spikeman —	ditto		
	Lieut. Kennedy —	ditto		
	Robert Avery — —	ditto		
	Thomas Brown —		ditto	
	Samuel Fisk — —	ditto		
	Serjeant Moore —			ditto
	John Cahall — —			ditto
	Total —	14	6	6

N. B. Those returned as Missing, we afterwards found, had been taken prisoners by the enemy.

Having

Having laid this return before Major Sparks, commanding officer at Fort Edward, he tranfmitted the fame to the General ; and the 30th of January following, I wrote to Capt. James Abercrombie, then at Albany, recommending fuch officers as I thought moft deferving, to fill up the vacancies occafioned by our late action, among whom were Lieutenant Stark to be Captain of Spikeman's company, and Serjeant Jofhua Martin to be Enfign in Captain Richard Rogers's company ; and I alfo mentioned feveral things in favour of the Rangers. In confequence whereof I received the following anfwer.

Dear Sir, *Albany, Feb.* 6, 1757.

" The General received your letter that was fent by Major Sparks, and returns you and your men thanks for their behaviour, and has recommended both you and them ftrongly to my Lord Loudoun, as alfo that they have payment for the prifoners they took. Upon receiving an account of your fkirmifh we fent an exprefs to Bofton, and, by the faid opportunity, recommended, for Spikeman's company,

pany, your brother * for a Lieutenant. We expect the exprefs back in a day or two, by whom, I dare fay, we fhall have my Lord's approbation of the Rangers. Pleafe to fend me the names of the officers you would recommend for your own company, and alfo to fill up the vacancies in the others; as I am certain you have the good of the fervice at heart, your recommendation will be paid great regard to. I yefterday received your's of the 30th of January. You cannot imagine how all ranks of people here are pleafed with your conduct, and your mens behaviour; for my part, it is no more than I expected: I was fo pleafed with their appearance when I was out with them, that I took it for granted they would behave well whenever they met the enemy. When I returned I reported them as fuch, and am glad they have anfwered my expectation.

"I am heartily forry for Spikeman and Kennedy, who I imagined would have turned out well, as likewife for the men you have loft; but it is impoffible to play at bowls without meeting with rubs. We muft try to revenge the lofs of them. There is few people that

* James Rogers.

will

will believe it; but, upon honour, I could be glad to have been with you, that I might have learned the manner of fighting in this country. The chance of being fhot is all ftuff, and King William's opinion and principle is much the beft for a foldier, viz. " that " every bullet has its billet," and that " it is " allotted how every man fhall die;" fo that I am certain that every one will agree, that it is better to die with the reputation of a brave man, fighting for his country in a good caufe, than either fhamefully running away to preferve one's life, or lingering out an old age, and dying in one's bed, without having done his country or his King any fervice.

" The hiftories of this country, particularly, are full of the unheard-of cruelties committed by the French, and the Indians, by their inftigation, which I think every brave man ought to do his utmoft to humble that haughty nation, or reduce their bounds of conqueft in this country to a narrow limit. As foon as General Abercrombie receives my Lord's inftructions in regard to the Rangers, I fhall fend you notice of it; in the interim, I hope you'll get the better of your wound. If I can be of any fervice to you or your men as long as they

continue

continue to behave fo well, you may command

Your moft humble fervant,

To Capt.   James Abercrombie,
Robert Rogers.   Aid de Camp."

My wound growing worfe, I was obliged to repair to Albany for better affiftance, and there received the following inftructions from General Abercrombie, viz.

Inftructions for Capt. ROBERT ROGERS.

" His Excellency the Earl of Loudoun having given authority to me to augment the company of Rangers under your command, to 100 men each, viz.

One Captain,
Two Lieutenants, } upon an Englifh pay ;
One Enfign,
Four Serjeants at 4s. each, New York currency ;
100 private men, at 2 s. and 6 d. each ditto per day ;

H   " And

" And whereas there are some private men of your company serving at present upon higher pay than the above establishment, you are at liberty to discharge them, in case they refuse to serve at the said establishment, as soon as you have other men to replace them. If your men agree to remain with you and serve upon the above establishment, you may assure them they will be taken notice of, and be first provided for ; each man to be allowed ten dollars bounty-money, and to find their own cloaths, arms, and blankets, and to sign a paper subjecting themselves to the rules and articles of war, and to serve during the war. You are to inlist no vagrants, but such as you and your officers are acquainted with, and who are every way qualified for the duty of Rangers ; and you and your officers are to use your best endeavours to complete your companies as soon as possible, and bring them to Fort Edward.

James Abercrombie,
Major General."

About this time I again wrote to his Lordship, earnestly soliciting his friendly interposition and assistance, to obtain from the government here, an order for payment of what

was

was due to me and my men, for our respective services during the winter 1755; but if that could not be obtained, that he would be pleased to direct me what method to take for recovery thereof. Whereto his Lordship replied, that as these services were antecedent to his command here, it was not in his power to reward them. General Amherst, afterwards, on a like application, gave me much the same answer.

These applications not being attended with any success, and suits of law being afterwards commenced against me, by, and on the behalf of those who served under me in that campaign, and verdicts obtained in their favour, I was not only obliged to answer their several demands, to the amount of £. 828 : 3 : 3 sterling, which I paid out of my private fortune, but also a considerable sum for law-charges, exclusive of what I ought to have received for my own services during that severe season. But for all which I have not at any time since received one shilling consideration.

In the same letter I likewise informed his Lordship of the death of Capt. Hobbs of the Rangers who died a few days before, and recommended Lieutenant Bulkley of the same

com-

company, as a proper perſon to ſucceed him in that command.

March 5, I was taken i l with the ſmall-pox, and not able to leave my room till the 15th of April following, during which time my officers were recruiting, agreeable to his Lordſhip's inſtructions. Not long after I received the following letter from Capt. Abercrombie.

Sir,   *New York, April* 22, 1757.

" As there is another ranging company ſent up to Albany, with orders to proceed to the forts, you will acquaint Colonel Gage, that it is my Lord Loudoun's orders, that the two companies at Fort William-Henry, and your own from Fort Edward, come down immediately to Albany, to be ready to embark for this place. Shew this letter to Colonel Gage, that he may acquaint Colonel Monro of his Lordſhip's orders, and that quarters may be provided for your companies in the houſes about Albany. You will take particular care that the companies have provided themſelves with all neceſſaries, and ſee that they are complete and good men. Since his Lordſhip has put it in your charge, I hope you will be very diligent in executing the truſt, for, upon a review

view of the men, if any are found infufficient for the fervice, the blame will be laid upon you. If the officers of this ranging company that is gone up, are not acquainted with the woods about Fort William-Henry, your brother muft fend fome officers and men of his company along with them, to let them know the different fcouts. I am, Sir,

Your moft humble fervant,

To Capt.   James Abercrombie,
Robert Rogers,   Aid de Camp."
   at Albany.

Capt. Richard Rogers, with his own, and the new company of Rangers before-mentioned, which was raifed in the Jerfies, and commanded by Capt. Burgin, being left at Fort William-Henry, my own company from Fort Edward, and Capt. Stark's and Capt. Bulkley's from Fort William-Henry, agreeable to the above inftructions, marched down to Albany, and from thence embarked for New York, where we were joined by another new-raifed company of Rangers, under the command of Capt. Shephard from New Hampfhire, and after fome fmall ftay there, re-embarked

barked on board a transport, and left Sandy
Hook on the 20th of June, with a fleet of near
an hundred sail, bound to Halifax, where
we soon arrived, and, according to orders, I
encamped on the Dartmouth-side of the harbour, while the army lay encamped on the
Halifax-side. The Rangers were here employed in various services.

On July 3d, by orders, I commanded a party to Lawrence Town, and from thence to
Schitzcook; some were left there to cut and
make up hay in the meadows, for the horses
intended to be used in an expedition to Louisburg; others covered the hay-makers, and o-
thers were dispatched on scouts, to make dis-
coveries; in one of which two deserters from
the 45th regiment were seized and brought in.

About the latter end of this month forty
Rangers were sent across the isthmus of Nova
Scotia, to the settlements on the Bay of Fun-
dy, and a party down to the north-west arm,
to scour the woods for deserters, &c. and
brought in several, both from the army and
navy.

About this time Admiral Holbourn arrived
with a fleet from England, with several regiments of regular troops on board, which were
landed, and likewise encamped at Halifax,

upon

upon which all scouting parties were called in; but certain intelligence being received that a French fleet of superior force had actually arrived at Louisburg, the intended expedition against that place was laid aside, and thereupon the Rangers were remanded back to the western frontiers.

Great numbers of the Rangers having been carried off this summer by the small-pox, I sent several of my officers, by his Lordship's command, to recruit in New Hampshire, and the Massachuset's provinces, with orders to join me at Albany. I afterwards embarked with the Rangers under my command, on board the fleet which carried the regular troops to New York, and from thence proceeded in small vessels up Hudson's River to Albany, where I was soon after joined by the new-raised recruits.

I then proceeded to Fort Edward, which was the only remaining cover to the northern frontiers of New York, and the more eastern provinces, Fort William-Henry * having been taken

---

* My brother Captain Richard Rogers died with the small-pox a few days before this fort was besieged; but such was the cruelty and rage of the enemy after their conquest, that they dug him up out of his grave, and scalped him. In

con-

taken by the French, under the command of Monſieur Montcalm, the Auguſt before. General Webb was then commanding officer at Fort Edward, and by his orders we were continually employed in patrolling the woods between this fort and Ticonderoga. In one of theſe parties, my Lord How did us the honour to accompany us, being fond, as he expreſſed himſelf, to learn our method of marching, ambuſhing, retreating, &c. and, upon our return, expreſſed his good opinion of us very generouſly.

About this time Lord Loudoun ſent the following volunteers in the regular troops, to be trained to the ranging, or wood-ſervice, under my command and inſpection; with particular orders to me to inſtruct them to the utmoſt of my power in the ranging-diſcipline, our methods of marching, retreating, ambuſhing, fighting, &c. that they might be the better qualified for any future ſervices againſt the enemy we had to contend with, deſiring me to take particular notice of each one's behaviour, and

conſequence of the articles of capitulation at the ſurrender of this fort, the two companies of Rangers there were diſbanded, and diſmiſſed the ſervice.

and to recommend them according to their several deserts, *viz.*

Walter Crofton
Mr. Lyshat   } of the 4th regiment
Mr. Roberts   of foot.

Charles Humbles
Richard Edlington
Andrew Crawley   } of the 22d ditto.
Thomas Millet

John Wilcox
John Wrightson
Michael Kent   } of the 27th ditto.
Mr. Monsel
Francis Creed

Alexander Robertson
William Frazier
John Graham
Andrew Ross
William Frazier, jun. } of the 42d ditto.
Archibald Campbell
Arch. Campbell, jun.
Augus. Campbell
Charles Menzies
John Robertson

I   Will.

Will. Ervin, or Irwin ⎫
Thomas Drought ⎪
William Drought ⎬ of the 44th ditto.
Francis Carruthers ⎪
John Clarke ⎭

Walter Paterson ⎫
Mr. Nicholson ⎪
Richard Boyce ⎬ of the 48th ditto.
Charles Perry ⎭

Mr. Christopher ⎫
Mr. Still ⎪
Mr. Hamilton ⎬ of the 55th ditto.
Mr. Young ⎭

Allen Grant ⎫ of the second batta-
Jonathan M‘Dougal ⎬ lion of Royal A-
Mr. Frisborough ⎭ mericans.

Nicholas Ward ⎫ of the 3d ditto.
James Hill ⎭

John

John Schlofer ⎫
George Wardoman ⎪
Francis Barnard ⎪
Engelbertus Horft ⎪
Ericke Reinhault ⎪
Andrew Wackerberg ⎬ of the 4th ditto.
Luhainfans Dekefar ⎪
Donald M'Bean ⎪
Henry Ven Bebber ⎪
John Boujour ⎭

Edward Crafton ⎫
James Pottinger ⎪
Simon Stephens ⎪
Archibald M'Donald ⎬ Rangers.
Hugh Sterling ⎪
Mr. Bridge ⎭

Thefe volunteers I formed into a company by themfelves, and took the more immediate command and management of them to my-felf; and for their benefit and inftruction re-duced into writing the following rules or plan of difcipline, which, on various occafions, I had found by experience to be neceffary and advantageous, viz.

I. All

I. All Rangers are to be fubject to the rules and articles of war; to appear at roll-call every evening on their own parade, equipped, each with a fire-lock, fixty rounds of powder and ball, and a hatchet, at which time an officer from each company is to infpect the fame, to fee they are in order, fo as to be ready on any emergency to march at a minute's warning; and before they are difmiffed the neceffary guards are to be draughted, and fcouts for the next day appointed.

II. Whenever you are ordered out to the enemies forts or frontiers for difcoveries, if your number be fmall, march in a fingle file, keeping at fuch a diftance from each other as to prevent one fhot from killing two men, fending one man, or more, forward, and the like on each fide, at the diftance of twenty yards from the main body, if the ground you march over will admit of it, to give the fignal to the officer of the approach of an enemy, and of their number, &c.

III. If you march over marfhes or foft ground, change your pofition, and march abreaft of each other, to prevent the enemy from tracking you, (as they would do if you

marched

marched in a single file) till you get over such ground, and then resume your former order, and march till it is quite dark before you encamp, which do, if possible, on a piece of ground that may afford your centries the advantage of seeing or hearing the enemy at some considerable distance, keeping one half of your whole party awake alternately through the night.

IV. Some time before you come to the place you would reconnoitre, make a stand, and send one or two men, in whom you can confide, to look out the best ground for making your observations.

V. If you have the good fortune to take any prisoners, keep them separate, till they are examined, and in your return take a different rout from that in which you went out, that you may the better discover any party in your rear, and have an opportunity, if their strength be superior to yours, to alter your course, or disperse, as circumstances may require.

VI. If you march in a large body of three or four hundred, with a design to attack the
enemy,

enemy, divide your party into three columns, each headed by a proper officer, and let thefe columns march in fingle files, the columns to the right and left keeping at twenty yards diſtance or more from that of the center, if the ground will admit, and let proper guards be kept in the front and rear, and fuitable flanking parties at a due diſtance as before directed, with orders to halt on all eminences, to take a view of the furrounding ground, to prevent your being ambufcaded, and to notify the approach or retreat of the enemy, that proper difpofitions may be made for attacking, defending, &c. And if the enemy approach in your front on level ground, form a front of your three columns or main body with the advanced guard, keeping out your flanking parties, as if you were marching under the command of trufty officers, to prevent the enemy from preffing hard on either of your wings, or furrounding you, which is the ufual method of the favages, if their number will admit of it, and be careful likewife to fupport and ftrengthen your rear-guard.

VII. If you are obliged to receive the enemy's fire, fall, or fquat down, till it is over, then rife and difcharge at them. If their main

body

body is equal to yours, extend yourfelves occa-
fionally; but if fuperior, be careful to fupport
and ftrengthen your flanking parties, to make
them equal with theirs, that if poffible you may
repulfe them to their main body, in which cafe
pufh upon them with the greateft refolution,
with equal force in each flank and in the
center, obferving to keep at a due diftance from
each other, and advance from tree to tree, with
one half of the party before the other ten or
twelve yards. If the enemy pufh upon you,
let your front fire and fall down, and then let
your rear advance thro' them and do the like,
by which time thofe who before were in front
will be ready to difcharge again, and repeat
the fame alternately, as occafion fhall require;
by this means you will keep up fuch a conftant
fire, that the enemy will not be able eafily to
break your order, or gain your ground.

VIII. If you oblige the enemy to retreat, be
careful, in your purfuit of them, to keep out
your flanking parties, and prevent them from
gaining eminences, or rifing grounds, in which
cafe they would perhaps be able to rally and
repulfe you in their turn.

IX.

IX. If you are obliged to retreat, let the front of your whole party fire and fall back, till the rear hath done the same, making for the best ground you can ; by this means you will oblige the enemy to pursue you, if they do it at all, in the face of a constant fire.

X. If the enemy is so superior that you are in danger of being surrounded by them, let the whole body disperse, and every one take a different road to the place of rendezvous appointed for that evening, which must every morning be altered and fixed for the evening ensuing, in order to bring the whole party, or as many of them as possible, together, after any separation that may happen in the day ; but if you should happen to be actually surrounded, form yourselves into a square, or if in the woods, a circle is best, and, if possible, make a stand till the darkness of the night favours your escape.

XI. If your rear is attacked, the main body and flankers must face about to the right or left, as occasion shall require, and form themselves to oppose the enemy, as before directed ; and the same method must be observed, if attacked in either of your flanks, by which

means

means you will always make a rear of one of your flank-guards.

XII. If you determine to rally after a retreat, in order to make a fresh stand against the enemy, by all means endeavour to do it on the most rising ground you can come at, which will give you greatly the advantage in point of situation, and enable you to repulse superior numbers.

XIII. In general, when pushed upon by the enemy, reserve your fire till they approach very near, which will then put them into the greater surprize and consternation, and give you an opportunity of rushing upon them with your hatchets and cutlasses to the better advantage.

XIV. When you encamp at night, fix your centries in such a manner as not to be relieved from the main body till morning, profound secrecy and silence being often of the last importance in these cases. Each centry, therefore, should consist of six men, two of whom must be constantly alert, and when relieved by their fellows, it should be done without noise; and in case those on duty see or hear any thing, which alarms them, they are not to speak, but

K   one

one of them is silently to retreat, and acquaint the commanding officer thereof, that proper dispositions may be made ; and all occasional centries should be fixed in like manner.

XV. At the first dawn of day, awake your whole detachment ; that being the time when the savages chuse to fall upon their enemies, you should by all means be in readiness to receive them.

XVI. If the enemy should be discovered by your detachments in the morning, and their numbers are superior to yours, and a victory doubtful, you should not attack them till the evening, as then they will not know your numbers, and if you are repulsed, your retreat will be favoured by the darkness of the night.

XVII. Before you leave your encampment, send out small parties to scout round it, to see if there be any appearance or track of an enemy that might have been near you during the night.

XVIII. When you stop for refreshment, chuse some spring or rivulet if you can, and dispose your party so as not to be surprised, post-

ing

ing proper guards and centries at a due diftance, and let a fmall party waylay the path
you came in, left the enemy fhould be purfuing.

XIX. If, in your return, you have to crofs
rivers, avoid the ufual fords as much as poffible, left the enemy fhould have difcovered,
and be there expecting you.

XX. If you have to pafs by lakes, keep at
fome diftance from the edge of the water, left,
in cafe of an ambufcade, or an attack from the
enemy, when in that fituation, your retreat
fhould be cut off.

XXI. If the enemy purfue your rear, take a
circle till you come to your own tracks,
and there form an ambufh to receive them,
and give them the firft fire.

XXII. When you return from a fcout, and
come near our forts, avoid the ufual roads, and
avenues thereto, left the enemy fhould have
headed you, and lay in ambufh to receive you,
when almoft exhaufted with fatigues.

K 2 XXIII.

XXIII. When you pursue any party that has been near our forts or encampments, follow not directly in their tracks, lest you should be discovered by their rear-guards, who, at such a time, would be most alert; but endeavour, by a different route, to head and meet them in some narrow pass, or lay in ambush to receive them when and where they least expect it.

XXIV. If you are to embark in canoes, battoes, or otherwise, by water, chuse the evening for the time of your embarkation, as you will then have the whole night before you, to pass undiscovered by any parties of the enemy, on hills, or other places, which command a prospect of the lake or river you are upon.

XXV. In padling or rowing, give orders that the boat or canoe next the sternmost, wait for her, and the third for the second, and the fourth for the third, and so on, to prevent separation, and that you may be ready to assist each other on any emergency.

XXVI. Appoint one man in each boat to look out for fires, on the adjacent shores, from the numbers and size of which you may form some

ſome judgment of the number that kindled them, and whether you are able to attack them or not.

XXVII. If you find the enemy encamped near the banks of a river, or lake, which you imagine they will attempt to croſs for their ſecurity upon being attacked, leave a detachment of your party on the oppoſite ſhore to receive them, while, with the remainder, you ſurprize them, having them between you and the lake or river.

XXVIII. If you cannot ſatisfy yourſelf as to the enemy's number and ſtrength, from their fire, &c. conceal your boats at ſome diſtance, and aſcertain their number by a reconnoitring party, when they embark, or march, in the morning, marking the courſe they ſteer, &c. when you may purſue, ambuſh, and attack them, or let them paſs, as prudence ſhall direct you. In general, however, that you may not be diſcovered by the enemy on the lakes and rivers at a great diſtance, it is ſafeſt to lay by, with your boats and party concealed all day, without noiſe or ſhew, and to purſue your intended route by night; and whether you go by land or water, give out parole and counter-

ſigns,

figns, in order to know one another in the
dark, and likewife appoint a ftation for every
man to repair to, in cafe of any accident that
may feparate you."

Such in general are the rules to be obferved
in the Ranging fervice; there are, however, a
thoufand occurrences and circumftances which
which may happen, that will make it neceffary, in fome meafure, to depart from them,
and to put other arts and ftratagems in prac-
tice; in which cafes every man's reafon and
judgment muft be his guide, according to the
particular fituation and nature of things; and
that he may do this to advantage, he fhould
keep in mind a maxim never to be departed
from by a commander, viz. to preferve a firm-
nefs and prefence of mind on every occafion.

My Lord Loudoun about this time made a
vifit to Fort Edward, and after giving directions for quartering the army the approaching
winter, left a ftrong garrifon there under the
command of Colonel Haviland, and returned
to Albany. The Rangers *, with the before-
mentioned

* Several of them were difmiffed with an allowance of
thirteen days pay to carry them home, being rendered unfit

mentioned volunteers, were encamped and quartered in huts on an adjacent island in Hudson's River, and were sent out on various scouts, in which my ill state of health at this time would not permit me to accompany them, till December 17, 1757, when, pursuant to orders from Lieutenant Colonel Haviland, commanding officer at Fort Edward, I marched from thence with a party of 150 men to reconnoitre Carillon, alias Ticonderoga, and if possible to take a prisoner. We marched six miles and encamped, the snow being then about three inches deep, and before morning it was fifteen: we however pursued our route.

On the 18th in the morning, eight of my party being tired, returned to the fort; with the remainder I marched nine miles further, and encamped on the east-side of Lake George, near the place where Monsanta. Montcalm landed his troops when he besieged and took Fort William-Henry, where I found some cannon-ball and shells, which had been hid by the French, and made a mark by which I might find them again.

fit for immediate service by their past fatigues, and several officers were sent recruiting in order to have the companies complete by the opening of the spring.

The

The 19th we continued our march on the weſt-ſide of the lake nine miles further, near the head of the north-weſt bay.

The 21ſt, ſo many of my party tired and returned as reduced our number to 123, officers included, with whom I proceeded ten miles further, and encamped at night, ordering each man to leave a day's proviſions there till our return.

The next day we marched ten miles further, and encamped near the great brook that runs into Lake George, eight miles from the French advanced guard.

The 23d we marched eight miles, and the 24th ſix more, and then halted within 600 yards of Carillon fort. Near the mills we diſcovered five Indian's tracks, that had marched that way the day before, as we ſuppoſed, on a hunting party. On my march this day between the advanced guard and the fort, I appointed three places of rendezvous to repair to, in caſe of being broke in an action, and acquainted every officer and ſoldier that I ſhould rally the party at the neareſt poſt to the fort, and if broke there to retreat to the ſecond, and at the third to make a ſtand till the darkneſs of the night would give us an opportunity to get off. Soon after I halted, I formed an ambuſh

on

on a road leading from the fort to the woods, with an advanced party of twenty men, and a rear-guard of fifteen. About eleven o'clock a ſerjeant of marines came from the fort up the road to my advanced party, who let him paſs to the main body, where I made him priſoner. Upon examination, he reported, " that there were in the garriſon 350 regulars, " about fifty workmen, and but five Indians : " that they had plenty of proviſions, &c. and " that twelve maſons were conſtantly em-" ployed in blowing up rocks in the en-" trenchment, and a number of ſoldiers to " aſſiſt them : that at Crown Point there " were 150 ſoldiers and fourteen Indians : " that Monſ. Montcalm was at Montreal : " that 500 Ottawawas Indians wintered in " Canada, and that 500 Rangers were lately " raiſed in Canada, each man having a double-" barrelled fuzee, and put under an experi-" enced officer, well acquainted with the " country : that he did not know whether the " French intended to attack any of the Eng-" liſh forts this winter or not; but that they " expected a great number of Indians as ſoon " as the ice would bear them, in order to go " down to the Engliſh forts; and that all the

L   " bakers

" bakers in Carillon were employed in baking
" bifcuit for the fcouts above-mentioned."

About noon, a Frenchman, who had been
hunting, came near my party in his return,
when I ordered a party to purfue him to the
edge of the cleared ground, and take him prifoner, with this caution, to fhoot off a gun or
two, and then retreat to the main body, in
order to intice the enemy from their fort ;
which orders were punctually obeyed, but
not one of them ventured out.

The laft prifoner, on examination, gave
much the fame account as the other, but with
this addition, " that he had heard the Englifh
" intended to attack Ticonderoga, as foon as
" the lake was froze fo as to bear them."

When I found the French would not come
out of the fort, we went about killing their
cattle, and deftroyed feventeen head, and fet
fire to the wood, which they had collected for
the ufe of the garrifon, and confumed five
large piles ; the French fhot off fome cannon
at the fires, but did us no harm. At eight
o'clock at night I began my march homewards, and arrived at Fort Edward with my
prifoners the 27th. In my return, I found at the
north-end of Lake George, where the
French had hid the boats they had taken at
Fort

Fort William Henry, with a great number of cannon-balls; but as the boats were under water we could not deſtroy them. Upon my return to Fort Edward, I received a letter from Captain Abercrombie, informing me that the Earl of Loudoun, who was then at New York, had thoughts of augmenting the Rangers, and had deſired General Abercrombie to command me down to receive his directions. I accordingly prepared for my journey, and upon my arrival was received by his Lordſhip in a very friendly manner; and, after much converſation upon the ſubject, he was pleaſed to inform me of his intentions of levying five additional companies of Rangers, deſiring me to name the perſons whom I thought fit for officers, and ſuch as might be depended upon, to levy the men his Lordſhip deſired; which I accordingly did, and then received from him the following inſtructions.

" By his Excellency John Earl of Loudoun, Lord Machline and Tairenſeen &c. &c. &c. one of the ſixteen peers of Scotland, Governor and Captain General of Virginia, and Vice Admiral of the ſame, Colonel of the 13th Regiment of foot, Colonel in chief of the Royal Ame-

rican

rican rigiment, Major General and Commander in Chief of all his Majesty's forces, raised or to be raised in North America:

" Whereas I have this day thought proper to augment the Rangers with five additional companies, that is, four New England and one Indian company, to be forthwith raised and employed in his Majesty's service; and whereas I have an entire confidence in your skill and knowledge, of the men most fit for that service; I do therefore, by these presents, appoint you to raise such a number of non-commission officers and private men as will be necessary to compleat the said five companies, upon the following establishment, viz. each company to confist of one Captain, two Lieutenants, one Ensign, four Serjeants, and 100 privates. The officers to have British pay, that is, the same as an officer of the like rank in his Majesty's regular forces; the Serjeants 4s. New York currency per day, and the private men 2s. 6d. currency per day. And the better to enable you to make this levy of men, you shall have one month's pay for each of the said five companies advanced to you; upon these conditions, that, out of the first warrants that

shall

ſhall hereafter be granted for the ſubſiſtence of theſe companies, ſhall be deducted the ſaid month's, pay now advanced. Your men to find their own arms, which muſt be ſuch as upon examination, ſhall be found fit, and be approved of. They are likewiſe to provide themſelves with good warm cloathing, which muſt be uniform in every company, and like-wiſe with good warm blankets. And the company of Indians to be dreſſed in all reſpects in the true Indian faſhion, and they are all to be ſubject to the rules and articles of war. You will forthwith acquaint the officers appointed to theſe companies, that they are immediately to ſet out on the recruiting ſervice, and you will not fail to inſtruct them that they are not to inliſt any man for a leſs term than one year, nor any but what are able-bodied, well acquainted with the woods, uſed to hunting, and every way qualified for the Rangeing ſervice. You are alſo to obſerve that the number of men requiſite to compleat the ſaid five companies, are all to be at Fort Edward on or before the 15th day of March next enſuing, and thoſe that ſhall come by the way of Albany are to be muſtered there by the officer commanding, as ſhall thoſe who go ſtrait to Fort Edward by the officer com-

manding

manding there. Given under my hand, at New York, the 11th day of January 1758.

Loudoun.

By his Excellency's command,

To Capt.   J. Appy."
Robert Rogers.

In pursuance of the above instructions, I immediately sent officers into the New England provinces, where, by the assistance of my friends, the requested augmentation of Rangers was quickly compleated, the whole five companies being ready for service by the 4th day of March.

Four of these companies were sent to Louisburg to join General Amherst, and one joined the corps under my command; and tho' I was at the whole expence of raising the five companies, I never got the least allowance for it, and one of the Captain's dying, to whom I had delivered a thousand dollars as advance pay for his company, which, agreeable to the instructions I received, I had a right to do; yet was I obliged to account with the government for this money, and entirely lost every penny of it.

It

It has already been mentioned, that the garrifon at Fort Edward was this winter under the command of Lieut. Col. Haviland. This gentleman, about the 28th of February, order-ed out a fcout under the direction of one Put-nam, Captain of a company of one of the Connecticut provincial regiments, with fome of my men, giving out publickly at the fame time, that, upon Putnam's return, I fhould be fent to the French forts with a ftrong party of 400 Rangers. This was known not only to all the officers, but foldiers alfo, at Fort Edward before Putnam's departure.

While this party was out, a fervant of Mr. Beft, a futler to the Rangers, was captivated by a flying party of the enemy from Ticonde-roga; unfortunately too, one of Putnam's men had left him at Lake George, and deferted to the enemy. Upon Captain Putnam's return, we were informed he had ventured within eight miles of the French fort at Ticonderoga, and that a party he had fent to make difcove-ries had reported to him, that there were near 600 Indians not far from the enemy's quarters.

March 10, 1758. Soon after the faid Captain Putnam's return, in confequence of pofitive orders from Col. Haviland, I this day began a march from Fort Edward for the neighbourhood

hood of Carillon, not with a party of 400 men, as at fi ft given out, but of 180 men only, officers included, one Captain, one Lieutenant, and one Enfign, and three volunteers, viz. Meff. Creed, Kent and Wrightfon, one ferjeant, and one private, all volunteers of the 27th regiment; and a detachment from the four companies of Rangers, quartered on the ifland near Fort Edward, viz. Capt. Bulkley, Lieutenants Philips, Moore, Crafton, Campbell, and Pottinger; Enfigns Rofs, Wait, McDonald, and White, and 162 private men. I acknowledge I entered upon this fervice, and viewed this fmall detachment of brave men march out, with no little concern and uneafinefs of mind; for as there was the greateft reafon to fufpect, that the French were, by the prifoner and deferter above mentioned, fully informed of the defign of fending me out upon Putman's return: what could I think! to fee my party, inftead of being ftrengthened and augmented, reduced to lefs than one half of the number at firft propofed. I muft confefs it appeared to me (ignorant and unfkilled as I then was in politicks and the arts of war) incomprehenfible; *but my commander doubtlefs had his reafons, and is able to vindicate his own conduct.* We marched to the half-way brook, in the road

leading

leading to Lake George, and there encamped the firſt night.

The 11th we proceeded as far as the firſt Narrows on Lake George, and encamped that evening on the eaſt-ſide of the lake; and after dark, I ſent a party three miles further down, to ſee if the enemy might be coming towards our forts, but they returned without diſcovering any. We were however on our guard, and kept parties walking on the lake all night, beſides centries at all neceſſary places on the land.

The 12th we marched from our encampment at ſun-riſe, and having diſtanced it about three miles, I ſaw a dog running acroſs the lake, whereupon I ſent a detachment to reconnoitre the iſland, thinking the Indians might have laid in ambuſh there for us; but no ſuch could be diſcovered; upon which I thought it expedient to put to ſhore, and lay by till night, to prevent any party from deſcrying us on the lake, from hills, or otherwiſe. We halted at a place called Sabbath-day Point, on the weſt-ſide of the lake, and ſent out parties to look down the lake with perſpective glaſſes, which we had for that purpoſe. As ſoon as it was dark we proceeded down the lake. I ſent Lieutenant Philips with fifteen

M   men

men, as an advanced guard, some of whom went before him on scates, while Ensign Ross flanked us on the left under the west-shore, near which we kept the main body, marching as close as possible, to prevent separation, it being a very dark night. In this manner we continued our march till within eight miles of the French advanced guards, when Lieutenant Philips sent a man on scates back to me, to desire me to halt; upon which I ordered my men to squat down upon the ice. Mr. Philips soon came to me himself, leaving his party to look out, and said, he imagined he had discovered a fire* on the east-shore, but was not certain; upon which I sent with him Ensign White, to make further discovery. In about an hour they returned, fully persuaded that a party of the enemy was encamped there. I then called in the advanced guard, and flanking party, and marched on to the west-shore, where, in a thicket, we hid our sleys and packs, leaving a small guard with them, and with the remainder I marched to attack

---

* A small party of the French, as we have since heard, had a fire here at this time; but, discovering my advanced party, extinguished their fire, and carried the news of our approach to the French fort.

the

the enemy's encampment, if there was any;
but when we came near the place, no fires
were to be seen, which made us conclude
that we had mistaken some bleach patches of
snow, or pieces of rotten wood, for fire (which
in the night, at a distance, resembles it) whereupon we returned to our packs, and there lay
the remainder of the night without fire.

The 13th, in the morning, I deliberated
with the officers how to proceed, who were
unanimously of opinion, that it was best to
go by land in snow-shoes, lest the enemy
should discover us on the lake; we accordingly continued our march on the west-side,
keeping on the back of the mountains that
overlooked the French advanced guards. At
twelve of the clock we halted two miles west
of those guards, and there refreshed ourselves
till three, that the day-scout from the fort
might be returned home before we advanced;
intending at night to ambuscade some of their
roads, in order to trepan them in the morning. We then marched in two divisions, the
one headed by Captain Bulkley, the other by
myself: Ensigns White and Wait had the
rear-guard, the other officers were posted properly in each division, having a rivulet at a

small

fmall diftance on our left, and a fteep mountain on our right. We kept clofe to the
mountain, that the advanced guard might
better obferve the rivulet, on the ice of which
I imagined they would travel if out, as the
fnow was four feet deep, and very bad travelling on fnow-fhoes. In this manner we
marched a mile and an half, when our advanced guard informed me of the enemy being in their view; and foon after, that they
had afcertained their number to be ninety-fix,
chiefly Indians. We immediately laid down
our packs, and prepared for battle, fuppofing
thefe to be the whole number or main body
of the enemy, who were marching on our left
up the rivulet, upon the ice. I ordered Enfign
M‘Donald to the command of the advanced
guard, which, as we faced to the left, made a
flanking party to our right. We marched to
within a few yards of the bank, which was
higher than the ground we occupied; and obferving the ground gradually to defcend from
the bank of the rivulet to the foot of the
mountain, we extended our party along the
bank, far enough to command the whole of
the enemy's at once; we waited till their front
was nearly oppofite to our left wing, when I
fired

fired a gun, as a fignal for a general difcharge upon them; whereupon we gave them the firft fire, which killed above forty Indians; the reft retreated, and were purfued by about one half of our people. I now imagined the enemy totally defeated, and ordered Enfign M Donald to head the flying remains of them, that none might efcape; but we foon found our miftake, and that the party we had attacked were only their advanced guard, their main body coming up, confifting of 600 more, Canadians and Indians; upon which I ordered our people to retreat to their own ground, which we gained at the expence of fifty men killed; the remainder I rallied, and drew up in pretty good order, where they fought with fuch intrepidity and bravery as obliged the enemy (tho' feven to one in number) to retreat a fecond time; but we not being in a condition to purfue them, they rallied again, and recovered their ground, and warmly pufhed us in front and both wings, while the mountain defended our rear; but they were fo warmly received, that their flanking parties foon retreated to their main body with confiderable lofs. This threw the whole again into diforder, and they retreated a third time;
but

but our number being now too far reduced to take advantage of their diforder, they rallied again, and made a freſh attack upon us. About this time we diſcovered 200 Indians going up the mountain on our right, as we ſuppoſed, to get poſſeſſion of the riſing ground, and attack our rear; to prevent which I ſent Lieutenant Philips, with eighteen men, to gain the firſt poſſeſſion, and beat them back; which he did: and being ſuſpicious that the enemy would go round on our left, and take poſſeſſion of the other part of the hill, I ſent Lieutenant Crafton, with fifteen men, to prevent them there; and ſoon after deſired two Gentlemen, who were volunteers in the party*, with a few men, to go and ſupport him, which they did with great bravery.

* I had before this deſired theſe Gentlemen to retire, offering them a Serjeant to conduct them; that as they were not uſed to ſnow-ſhoes, and were quite unacquainted with the woods, they wou'd have no chance of eſcaping the enemy, in caſe we ſhould be broke and put to flight, which I very much ſuſpected. They at firſt ſeemed to accept the offer, and began to retire; but ſeeing us ſo cloſely beſet, they undauntedly returned to our aſſiſtance. What befel them after our flight, may be ſeen by a letter from one of the Gentlemen to the commanding officer, which I have inſerted next to this account of our ſcout.

The

The enemy pufhed us fo clofe in front, that the parties were not more than twenty yards afunder in general, and fometimes intermixed with each other. The fire continued almoft conftant for an hour and half from the beginning of the attack, in which time we loft eight officers, and more than 100 private men killed on the fpot. We were at laft obliged to break, and I with about twenty men ran up the hill to Philips and Crafton, where we ftopped and fired on the Indians, who were eagerly pufhing us, with numbers that we could not withftand. Lieutenant Philips being furrounded by 300 Indians, was at this time capitulating for himfelf and party, on the other part of the hill. He fpoke to me, and faid if the enemy would give them good quarters, he thought it beft to furrender, otherwife that he would fight while he had one man left to fire a gun †.

I now thought it moft prudent to retreat, and bring off with me as many of my party as I poffibly could, which I immediately did; the Indians clofely purfuing us at the fame time, took

---

† This unfortunate officer, and his whole party, after they furrendered, upon the ftrongeft affurances of good treatment from the enemy, were inhumanly tied up to trees, and hewn to pieces, in a moft barbarous and fhocking manner.

feveral

several prisoners. We came to Lake George in the evening, where we found several wounded men, whom we took with us to the place where we had left our sleds, from whence I sent an express to Fort Edward, desiring Mr. Haviland to send a party to meet us, and assist in bringing in the wounded; with the remainder I tarried there the whole night, without fire or blankets, and in the morning we proceeded up the lake, and met with Captain Stark at Hoop Island, six miles north from Fort William-Henry, and encamped there that night; the next day being the 15th, in the evening, we arrived at Fort Edward.

The number of the enemy was about 700, 600 of which were Indians. By the best accounts we could get, we killed 150 of them, and wounded as many more. I will not pretend to determine what we should have done had we been 400 or more strong; but this I am obliged to say of those brave men who attended me (most of whom are now no more) both officers and soldiers in their respective stations behaved with uncommon resolution and courage; nor do I know an instance during the whole action in which I can justly impeach the prudence or good conduct of any one of them.

The

The following is a L I S T of the Killed, Missing, &c.

The Captain and Lieutenant of his Majesty's regular troops, volunteers in this party, were taken prisoners; the Ensign, another volunteer of the same corps, was killed, as were two volunteers, and a Serjeant of the said corps, and one private.

Of Capt. Rogers's Company,

    Lieut. Moore   —   Killed.
    Serjeant Parnell   —   Ditto.
    Thirty-six privates   Ditto.

Of Capt. Shepherd's Company,

    Two Serjeants
    Sixteen privates

Of Capt. James Rogers's Company,

    Ensign M'Donald   —   Killed.

Of Capt. John Starks's Company,

    Two Serjeants   —   Killed.
    Fourteen privates   Ditto.

Of

Of Capt. Bulkley's Company,

Capt. Bulkley	—	Killed.
Lieut. Pottinger	—	Ditto.
Enſign White	—	Ditto.
Forty-ſeven privates	—	K. and Miſſ.

Of Capt. William Starks's Company,

Enſign Roſs	—	Killed.

Of Capt. Brewer's Company,

Lieut. Campbell	Killed.

A Gentleman of the army, who was a volunteer on this party, and who with another
fell into the hands of the French, wrote the
following letter, ſome time after, to the officer
commanding the regiment they belonged to at
Fort Edward.

Carillon, March 28, 1758.

" Dear Sir,

" As a flag of truce is daily expeɕted here with
an anſwer to Monſieur Vaudreuil, I ſit down
to

to write the moment I am able, in order to have
a letter ready, as no doubt you and our friends
at Fort Edward are anxious to be informed
about Mr. ———— and me, whom probably
you have reckoned amongſt the ſlain in our
unfortunate rencontre of the 13th concerning which at preſent I ſhall not be particular ;
only to do this juſtice to thoſe who loſt their
lives there, and to thoſe who have eſcaped, to
aſſure you, Sir, that ſuch diſpoſitions were
formed by the enemy, (who diſcovered us long
enough before) it was impoſſible for a party ſo
weak as ours to hope for even a retreat.   Towards the concluſion of the affair, it was cried
from a riſing ground on our right, to retire
there ; where, after ſcrambling with difficulty,
as I was unaccuſtomed to ſnow-ſhoes, I found
Capt. Rogers, and told him, that I ſaw to retire further was impoſſible, therefore earneſtly
begged we might collect all the men left, and
make a ſtand there.   Mr. ————, who was
with him, was of my opinion, and Capt.
Rogers alſo ; who therefore deſired me to
maintain one ſide of the hill, whilſt he defended the other.   Our parties did not exceed above
ten or twelve in each, and mine was ſhifting
towards the mountain, leaving me unable to
defend my poſt, or to labour with them up the
hill.

hill. In the mean time, Capt. Rogers with his party came to me, and said (as did all those with him) that a large body of Indians had ascended to our right; he likewise added, what was true, that the combat was very unequal, that I must retire, and he would give Mr. —— and me a Serjeant to conduct us thro' the mountain. No doubt prudence required us to accept his offer; but, besides one of my snow-shoes being untied, I knew myself unable to march as fast as was requisite to avoid becoming a sacrifice to an enemy we could no longer oppose; I therefore begged of him to proceed, and then leaned against a rock in the path, determined to submit to a fate I thought unavoidable. Unfortunately for Mr. —— his snow shoes were loosened likewise, which obliged him to determine with me, not to labour in a flight we were both unequal to. Every instant we expected the savages; but what induced them to quit this path, in which we actually saw them, we are ignorant of, unless they changed it for a shorter, to intercept those who had just left us. By their noise, and making a fire, we imagined they had got the rum in the Rangers packs. This thought, with the approach of night, gave us the first hopes of retiring; and when the moon arose,

we

we marched to the fouthward along the mountains about three hours, which brought us to
ice, and gave us reafon to hope our difficulties
were almoft paft; but we knew not we had
enemies yet to combat with, more cruel than
the favages we had efcaped. We marched all
night, and on the morning of the 14th found
ourfelves entirely unacquainted with the ice.
Here we faw a man, who came towards us; he
was the fervant of Capt. Rogers, with whom
he had been oftentimes all over the country,
and, without the leaft hefitation whatfoever, he
informed us we were upon South-Bay; that
Wood-Creek was juft before us; that he knew
the way to Fort Anne extremely well, and
would take us to Fort Edward the next day.
Notwithftanding we were difappointed in our
hopes of being upon Lake George, we thought
ourfelves fortunate in meeting fuch a guide, to
whom we gave entire confidence, and which
he in fact confirmed, by bringing us to a creek,
where he fhewed the tracks of Indians, and the
path he faid they had taken to Fort Anne.
After ftruggling thro' the fnow fome hours, we
were obliged to halt to make fnow-fhoes,
as Mr. —— and the guide had left theirs at
arriving upon the ice. Here we remained all
night, without any blankets, no coat, and but a
                                        fingle

single waistcoat each, for I gave one of mine to Mr. ———, who had laid aside his green jacket in the field, as I did likewise my furred cap, which became a mark to the enemy, and probably was the cause of a slight wound in my face; so that I had but a silk handkerchief on my head, and our fire could not be large, as we had nothing to cut wood with. Before morning we contrived, with forked sticks and strings of leather, a sort of snow-shoes, to prevent sinking entirely; and, on the 15th, followed our guide west all day, but he did not fulfil his promise; however the next day it was impossible to fail: but even then, the 16th, he was unsuccessful; yet still we were patient, because he seemed well acquainted with the way, for he gave every mountain a name, and shewed us several places, where he said his master had either killed deer or encamped. The ground, or rather the want of sun-shine, made us incline to the southward, from whence by accident we saw ice, at several miles distance, to the south-east. I was very certain, that, after marching two days west of South Bay, Lake George could not lie south-east from us, and therefore concluded this to be the upper end of the bay we had left. For this reason, together with the assurances of our guide, I advised

continuing

continuing our courfe to the weft, which muft
fhortly ftrike Fort Anne, or fome other place
that we knew. But Mr —— wifhed to be
upon ice at any rate; he was unable to continue
in the fnow, for the difficulties of our march
had overcome him. And really, Sir, was I to
be minute in thofe we had experienced already
and afterwards, they would almoft be as tire-
fome to you to read, as they were to us to fuffer.

Our fnow-fhoes breaking, and finking to
our middle every fifty paces, the fcrambling
up mountains, and acrofs fallen timber, our
nights without fleep or covering, and but little
fire, gathered with great fatigue, our fuftenance
moftly water, and the bark and berries of
trees; for all our provifions from the beginning was only a fmall Bologna faufage, and a
little ginger, I happened to have, and which
even now was very much decreafed; fo that I
knew not how to oppofe Mr. ——'s intreaties;
but as our guide ftill perfifted Fort Anne was
near, we concluded to fearch a little longer,
and if we made no difcovery to proceed next
day towards the ice; but we fought in vain, as
did our guide the next morning, tho' he returned, confidently afferting he had difcovered
frefh proofs, that the fort could not be far off.
I confefs I was ftill inclined to follow him, for
                                        I was

I was almoſt certain the beſt we could hope
from deſcending upon this ice to our left, was
to throw ourſelves into the hands of the
French, and perhaps not be able to effect even
that; but, from the circumſtances I have mentioned, it was a point I muſt yield to, which I
did with great reluctancy. The whole day of
the 17th we marched a dreadful road, between the mountains, with but one good ſnow-
ſhoe each, the other of our own making being
almoſt uſeleſs. The 18th brought us to the ice,
which tho' we longed to arrive at, yet I ſtill
dreaded the conſequence, and with reaſon, for
the firſt ſight informed us, it was the very place
we had left five days before. Here I muſt
own my reſolution almoſt failed me; when fatigue, cold, hunger, and even the proſpect of
periſhing in the woods attended us, I ſtill had
hopes, and ſtill gave encouragement, but now
I wanted it myſelf; we had no reſource but to
throw ourſelves into the enemy's hands, or
periſh. We had nothing to eat, our ſlender
ſtock had been equally ſhared amongſt us
three, and we were not ſo fortunate as ever to
ſee either bird or beaſt to ſhoot at. When
our firſt thoughts were a little calmed, we
conceived hopes, that, if we appeared before
the French fort, with a white flag, the commanding

manding officer would relieve and return us to Fort Edward. This served to palliate our neareſt approach to deſpair, and determined a reſolution, where, in fact, we had no choice. I knew Carillon had an extenſive view up South Bay, therefore we concluded to halt during the evening, and march in the night, that we might approach it in the morning, beſides the wind pierced us like a ſword; but inſtead of its abating it increaſed, together with a freezing rain, that incruſted us entirely with ice, and obliged us to remain until morning, the 19th, when we fortunately got ſome juniper berries, which revived, gave us ſpirits, and I thought ſtrength. We were both ſo firmly of that opinion, that we propoſed taking the advantage of its being a dark ſnowy day, to approach Carillon, to paſs it in the night, and get upon Lake George. With difficulty we perſuaded the guide to be of our opinion, we promiſed large rewards in vain, until I aſſured him of proviſions hid upon the lake; but we little conſidered how much nature was exhauſted, and how unequal we were to the taſk: however, a few miles convinced us we were ſoon midway up our legs in the new-fallen ſnow; it drove full in our faces, and was as dark as the fogs upon the banks of

New-

Newfoundland. Our ſtrength and our hopes
ſunk together, nay, even thoſe of reaching
Carillon were doubtful, but we muſt proceed
or periſh. As it cleared up a little, we laboured to ſee the fort, which at every turn we
expected, until we came to where the ice was
gone, and the water narrow. This did not a-
gree with my idea of South Bay, but it was no
time for reflection; we quitted the ice to the
left, and after marching two miles, our guide
aſſured us we ought to be on the other ſide of
the water. This was a very diſtreſſing circum-
ſtance, yet we returned to the ice and paſſed
to the right, where, after ſtruggling through
the ſnow, about four miles, and breaking in
every ſecond ſtep, as we had no ſnow-ſhoes,
we were ſtopped by a large water-fall. Here
I was again aſtoniſhed with appearances, but
nothing now was to be thought of only reaching the fort before night; yet to paſs this
place ſeemed impracticable: however, I attempted to ford it a little higher, and had almoſt gained the oppoſite ſhore, where the
depth of the water, which was up to my
breaſt, and the rapidity of the ſtream, hurried
me off the ſlippery rocks, and plunged me
entirely in the waters. I was obliged to quit
my fuzee, and with great difficulty eſcaped
being

being carried down the fall. Mr. ———, who followed me, and the guide, though they held by one another, fuffered the fame fate; but the hopes of foon reaching a fire made us think lightly of this: as night approached, we laboured exceffively through the fnow; we were certain the fort was not far from us, but our guide confeffed, for the firft time, that he was at a lofs. Here we plainly obferved that his brain was affected: he faw Indians all around him, and though we have fince learned we had every thing to fear from them, yet it was a danger we did not now attend to; nay, we fhouted aloud feveral times to give information we were there; but we could neither hear nor fee any body to lead us right, or more likely to deftroy us, and if we halted a minute we became pillars of ice; fo that we refolved, as it froze fo hard, to make a fire, although the danger was apparent. Accidentally we had one dry cartridge, and in trying with my piftol if it would flafh a little of the powder, Mr. ——— unfortunately held the cartridge too near, by which it took fire, blew up in our faces, almoft blinded him, and gave exceffive pain. This indeed promifed to be the laft ftroke of fortune, as our hopes of a fire were now no more; but al-

though

though we were not anxious about life, we knew it was more becoming to oppofe than yield to this laft misfortune. We made a path round a tree, and there exercifed all the night, though fcarcely able to ftand, or prevent each other from fleeping. Our guide, notwithftanding repeated cautions, ftraggled from us, where he fat down and died immediately. On the morning of the 20th, we faw the fort, which we approached with a white flag : the officers run violently towards us, and faved us from a danger we did not then apprehend ; for we are informed, that if the Indians, who were clofe after them, had feized us firft, it would not have been in the power of the French to have prevented our being hurried to their camp, and perhaps to Montreal the next day, or killed for not being able to march. Monf. Debecourt and all his officers treat us with humanity and politenefs, and are folicitous in our recovery, which returns flowly, as you may imagine, from all thefe difficulties ; and though I have omitted many, yet I am afraid you will think me too prolix ; but we wifh, Sir, to perfuade you of a truth, that nothing but the fituation I have faithfully defcribed could determine us in a

refolu-

refolution which appeared only one degree
preferable to perifhing in the woods.

"I fhall make no comments upon thefe diftreffes; the malicious perhaps will fay, which
is very true, we brought them upon ourfelves;
but let them not wantonly add, we deferved
them becaufe we were unfuccefsful. They
muft allow we could not be led abroad, at
fuch a feafon of fnow and ice, for amufement,
or by an idle curiofity. I gave you, Sir, my
reafons for afking leave, which you were
pleafed to approve, and I hope will defend
them; and the fame would make me again,
as a volunteer, experience the chance of war
to-morrow, had I an opportunity. Thefe are
Mr. ———'s fentiments as well as mine; and
we both know you, Sir, too well, to harbour
the leaft doubt of receiving juftice with regard
to our conduct in this affair, or our promotion in the regiment; the profpect of not
joining that fo foon as we flattered ourfelves
has depreffed our fpirits to the loweft degree,
fo that we earneftly beg you will be folicitous
with the General to have us reftored as foon
as poffible, or at leaft to prevent our being
fent to France, and feparated from you, perhaps, during the war.

I have

I have but one thing more to add, which we learned here, and which perhaps you have already obferved from what I have faid, that we were upon no other ice than that of Lake George; but by the day overtaking us, the morning of the 14th, in the very place we had, in coming, marched during the night, we were entirely unacquainted with it, and obliged to put a confidence in this guide, whofe head muft have been aftray from the beginning, or he could not fo grofsly have miftaken a place where he had fo often been. This information but added to our diftrefs, until we reflected that our not being entirely loft was the more wonderful. That we had parted from South Bay on the 14th, was a point with us beyond all doubt, and about which we never once hefitated, fo that we acted entirely contrary to what we had eftablifhed as a truth; for if, according to that, we had continued our courfe to the weft, we muft inevitably have perifhed; but the hand of Providence led us back contrary to our judgment; and though even then, and often afterwards, we thought it fevere, yet in the end it faved us, and obliged us to reft fatisfied that we conftrued many things unfortunate, which tended to our prefervation.   I am, &c."

Upon

Upon my return from the late unfortunate scout, I was ordered to Albany to recruit my companies, where I met with a very friendly reception from my Lord How, who advanced me cash to recruit the Rangers, and gave me leave to wait upon General Abercrombie at New York, who had now succeeded my Lord Loudoun in the chief command, my Lord being at this time about to embark for England. I here received a commission from the General, of which the following is a copy.

" By his Excellency James Abercromby, Esq; Colonel of his Majesty's 44th Regiment of Foot, Colonel in Chief of the 60th or Royal American Regiment, Major General and Commander in Chief of all his Majesty's Forces raised or to be raised in North America, &c.

" Whereas it may be of great use to his Majesty's service in the operations now carrying on for recovering his rights in America, to have a number of men employed in obtaining intelligence of the strength, situation, and motions of the enemy, as well as other services, for which Rangers, or men acquainted with the woods, only are fit: Having the
greatest

greateſt confidence in your loyalty, courage and ſkill in this kind of ſervice, I do, by vir- of the power and authority to me given by his Majeſty, hereby conſtitute and appoint you to be Major of the Rangers in his Majeſty's ſervice, and likewiſe Captain of a company of ſaid Rangers. You are therefore to take the ſaid Rangers as Major, and the ſaid Company as Captain, into your care and charge, and duly exerciſe and inſtruct, as well the officers as the ſoldiers thereof, in arms, and to uſe your beſt endeavours to keep them in good order and diſcipline; and I do hereby command them to obey you as their Major and Captain reſpectively, and you are to follow and ob- ſerve ſuch orders and directions from time to time as you ſhall receive from his Majeſty, myſelf, or any other ſuperior officer, according to the rules and diſcipline of war.

Given at New York, this 6th Day of April 1758, in the thirty-firſt Year of the reign of our Sovereign Lord George the Second, by the Grace of God, King of Great Britain, France and Ireland, Defender of the Faith, &c.

JAMES ABERCROMBY.

By his Excellency's command,

J. APPY."

I left

I left New York April 8, and according
to orders attended Lord How at Albany,
for his directions, on the 12th, with whom I
had a moſt agreeable interview, and a long
converſation concerning the methods of diſtreſſing the enemy, and proſecuting the war
with vigour the enſuing campaign. I parted
with him, having the ſtrongeſt aſſurances of
his friendſhip and influence in my behalf, to
wait upon Colonel Grant, commanding officer
at Fort Edward, to aſſiſt him in conducting
the Rangers, and ſcouting parties, in ſuch a
manner as might beſt ſerve the common
cauſe, having a letter from my Lord to him.
Capt. Stark was immediately diſpatched to
Ticonderoga on the weſt-ſide of Lake George.
Capt. Jacob, whoſe Indian name was *Naw-
nawapeteoonks*, on the eaſt-ſide, and Capt.
Shepherd betwixt the lakes, with directions to
take if poſſible ſome priſoners near Carillon.
About the ſame time I marched myſelf with
eighteen men for Crown Point. Capt. Burbank was likewiſe diſpatched in queſt of priſoners. Theſe ſcouts, being often relieved,
were kept out pretty conſtantly, in order to
diſcover any parties of the enemy that might
ſally out towards our forts or frontiers, and to

P

reconnoitre

reconnoitre their situation and motions from time to time. The success of my own scout was as follows.

April 29, 1758, I marched from Fort Edward with a party of eighteen men, up the road that leads to Fort William Henry four miles, then north four miles, and encamped at Schoon Creek, it having been a very rainy day.

On the 30th we marched north-and-by-east all day, and encamped near South-Bay.

The 1st of May we continued the same course, and at night encamped near the narrows, north of South Bay.

The 2d, in the morning, made a raft, and crossed the bay over to the east-side, and having distanced the lake about four miles we encamped.

The 3d we steered our course north, and lay at night about three miles from Carillon.

The 4th we marched north-by-east all day, and encamped at night three miles from Crown Point Fort.

The 5th we killed one Frenchman, and took three prisoners.

The 6th, in the morning, began our return homeward, and arrived with our prisoners at Fort Edward the 9th.

One

One of the prisoners, who appeared to be the most intelligible, reported, " that he was born " at Lorrain in France; that he had been in " Canada eight years, viz two at Quebec, one " at Montreal, and five at Crown Point; that " at the latter were but 200 soldiers, of which " Monf. le Janong was commander in chief; " that at Ticonderoga there were 400 of the " Queen's regiment, 150 marines, 200 Cana- " dians, and about 700 Indians; and that they " daily expected 300 Indians more; that they " did not intend to attack our forts this fum- " mer, but were preparing to receive us at " Ticonderoga; that they had heard that I, " with most of my party, was killed in the " conflict laft March; but afterwards, by fome " prisoners which a fmall party of their Indi- " ans had taken from Dutch Hoofyk, they were " informed that Rogers was yet alive, and was " going to attack them again, being fully re- " folved to revenge the inhumanity and bar- " barity with which they had ufed his men, " in particular Lieut. Philips and his party, " who were butchered by them, after they had " promifed them quarters; that this was talked " of among the Indians, who greatly blamed " the French for encouraging them fo to do."

P 2

Captains

Captains Stark and Jacob returned the day before me; the former brought in with him six prisoners, four of which he took near Ticonderoga; they having escaped from New York and Albany, were in their flight to the French forts. The latter, who had but one white man with him, and eighteen Indians, took ten prisoners, and seven scalps, out of a party of fifty French. An account of these scouts, and the intelligence thereby gained, was transmitted to my Lord How, and by him to the General.

About the middle of May, a flag of truce was sent to Ticonderoga, on Col. Schyler's account, which put a stop to all offensive scouts, till its return.

May 28, 1758, I received positive orders from the General, to order all officers and men, belonging to the Rangers, and the two Indian companies, who were on furlow, or recruiting parties, to join their respective companies as soon as possible, and that every man of the corps under my command should be at his post at or before the 10th of next month. These orders were obeyed, and parties kept out on various scouts till the 8th of June, when my Lord How arrived at Fort Edward with one half of the army.

His

His Lordſhip immediately ordered me out with fifty men in whale-boats, which were carried over in waggons to Lake George, and directed me at all events to take a plan of the landing-place at the north-end with all poſſible accuracy, and alſo of the ground from the landing-place to the French fort at Carillon, and of Lake Champlain for three miles beyond it, and to diſcover the enemy's number in that quarter. Agreeable to theſe orders, on the 12th in the morning, I marched with a party of fifty men, and encamped in the evening at the place where Fort William Henry ſtood.

On the 30th we proceeded down the lake in five whale-boats to the firſt narrows, and ſo on to the weſt-end of the lake, where I took the plan his Lordſhip deſired. Part of my party then proceeded to reconnoitre Ticonderoga, and diſcovered a large encampment there, and a great number of Indians. While I was, with two or three others, taking a plan of the fort, encampment, &c. I left the remainder of my party at ſome conſiderable diſtance; when I was returning to them, at the diſtance of about 300 yards, they were fallen upon by a ſuperior number of the enemy who had got between me and them. Capt. Jacobs, with the Mohegon Indians, run off at the firſt onſet,

calling

calling to our people to run likewise; but they
stood their ground, and discharged their pieces
several times. at last broke through the enemy,
by whom they were surrounded on all sides
except their rear, where a river covered them:
they killed three of the enemy, but lost eight
of their own party in this skirmish. My party
rallied at the boats, where I joined them, and
having collected all but the slain together,
we returned homewards. On the 20th,
at Half Way brook, we met my Lord How,
advanced with three thousand men, to whom I
gave an account of my scout, together with a
plan of the landing-place, the fort at Carillon,
and the situation of the lakes.

I obtained leave of my Lord to go to Fort
Edward, where his Excellency Major General
Abercrombie was then posted, who ordered
me to join my Lord How the next day with
all the Rangers, being 600, in order to proceed with his Lordship to the lake.

On the 22d his Lordship encamped at the
lake where formerly stood Fort William-Henry, and ordered the Rangers to advance 400
yards on the west-side, and encamp there;
from which place, by his Lordship's orders, I
sent off next morning three small parties of
Rangers, viz. one to the narrows of South
Bay,

Bay, another to the weft-fide of Lake George, and a third to Ticonderoga Fort, all three parties by land. Another party, confifting of two Lieutenants and feventeen men, proceeded down the lake for difcoveries, and were all made prifoners by about 300 French and Indians. This party embarked in whale-boats.

About the 28th of June his Excellency Major General Abercrombie arrived at the lake with the remainder of the army, where he tarried till the morning of the 5th of July, and then the whole army, confifting of near 16,000, embarked in battoes for Ticonderoga.

The order of march was a moft agreeable fight; the regular troops in the center, provincials on each wing, the light infantry on the right of the advanced guard, the Rangers on the left, with Colonel Broadftreet's battoemen in the center. In this manner we proceeded, till dufk, down Lake George, to Sabbath Day Point, where the army halted and refrefhed. About ten o'clock the army moved again, when my Lord How went in the front with his whale-boat, Lieutenant Col. Broadftreet's and mine, with Lieutenant Holmes, in another, whom he fent forward to go near the landing-place, and obferve if any enemy was pofted there.

Holmes

Holmes returned about day-break, met the army near the Blue Mountains within four miles of the landing-place, and reported that there was a party of the enemy at the landing-place, which he difcovered by their fires.

As foon as it was light his Lordfhip, with Col. Broadftreet and myfelf, went down to obferve the landing-place before the army, and when within about a quarter of a mile, plainly difcerned that it was but a fmall detachment of the enemy that was there; whereupon his Lordfhip faid he would return to the General, that the army might land and march to Ticonderoga. About twelve o'clock the whole army landed, the Rangers on the left wing. I immediately fent an officer to wait upon the General for his orders, and received directions from Capt. Abercrombie, one of his Aids de Camp, to gain the top of a mountain that bore north about a mile from the landing-place, and from thence to fteer eaft to the river that runs into the falls betwixt the landing and the faw-mill, to take poffeffion of fome rifing ground on the enemy's fide, and there to wait the army's coming. I immediately marched, afcended the top of the hill, and from thence marched to the place I was ordered, where I arrived in about

an

an hour, and posted my party to as good advantage as I could, being within one quarter of a mile of where Monf. Montcalm was posted with 1500 men, whom I had discovered by some small reconnoitring parties sent out for that purpose. About twelve o'clock Colonels Lyman and   tch of the Provincials came to my rear, whom I informed of the enemy's being so very near, and inquiring concerning the army, they told me they were coming along. While this conversation passed, a sharp fire began in the rear of Col. Lyman's regiment, on which he said he would make his front immediately, and desired me to fall on their left flank, which I accordingly did, having first ordered Capt. Burbanks with 150 men to remain at the place where I was posted, to observe the motions of the French at the saw-mills, and went with the remainder of the Rangers on the left flank of the enemy, the river being on their right, and killed several. By this time my Lord Howe, with a detachment from his front, had broke the enemy, and hemmed them in on every side; but advancing himself with great eagerness and intrepidity upon them, was unfortunately shot

Q   and

and died immediately *. There were taken prisoners of the enemy in this action, five officers, two volunteers, and one hundred and sixty men, who were sent to the landing place. Nothing more material was done this day. The next morning, at six o'clock, I was ordered to march to the river that runs into the falls, the place where I was the day before, and there to halt on the west-side till further orders, with four hundred Rangers, while Captain Stark, with the remainder of the Rangers, marched with Capt. Abercombie and Mr. Clerk the Engineer to observe the position of the enemy at the fort, from whence they returned again that evening. The whole army lay the ensuing night under arms. By sunrise next morning, Sir William Johnson joined the army with four hundred and forty Indians. At seven o'clock I received orders to march with my Rangers. A Lieutenant of Captain Stark's led the advance guard. I was within about three hundred yards of the breast-work, when my advance guard was ambushed and

* This noble and brave officer being universally beloved by both officers and soldiers of the army, his fall was not only most sincerely lamented, but seemed to produce an almost general consternation and languor through the whole.

fired

fired upon by about 200 Frenchmen. I immediately formed a front, and marched up to the advanced guard, who maintained their ground, and the enemy immediately retreated; soon after the battoe-men formed on my left and light infantry on my right. This fire of the enemy did not kill a single man. Soon after three regiments of Provincials came up and formed in my rear, at two hundred yards distance. While the army was thus forming, a scattering fire was kept up between our flying parties and those of the enemy without the breast-work. About half an hour past ten, the greatest part of the army being drawn up, a smart fire began on the left wing, where Col. De Lancey's, (the New Yorkers,) and the battoe-men were posted, upon which I was ordered forward to endeavour to beat the enemy within the breast-work, and then to fall down, that the pickets and grenadiers might march through. The enemy soon retired within their works; Major Proby marched through with his pickets within a few yards of the breast-work, where he unhappily fell, and the enemy keeping up a heavy fire, the soldiers hastened to the right about, when Col. Haldiman came up with the granadiers to support them, being followed by the battali-

ons

ons in brigades for their support. Col. Haldiman advanced very near the breast work,
which was at least eight feet high ; some of
the provincials with the Mohocks came up
also *.

We toiled with repeated attacks for four
hours, being greatly embarrassed by trees that
were felled by the enemy without their breast-
work, when the General thought proper to
order a retreat, directing me to bring up the
rear, which I did in the dusk of the evening.
On the ninth in the evening, we arrived at
our encampment at the south-end of Lake
George, where the army received the thanks
of the General for their good behaviour, and
were ordered to entrench themselves ; the
wounded were sent to Fort Edward and Albany.   Our loss both in the regular and provincial troops, was somewhat considerable.
The enemy's loss was about five hundred, besides those who were taken prisoners.

July 8, 1758. By order of the General, I
this day began a scout to South Bay, from

* This attack was begun before the General intended
it should be, and as it were by accident, from the fire of
the New Yorkers in the left wing ; upon which Col. Haviland being in or near the center, ordered the troops to
advance.

which

which I returned the 16th, having effected nothing confiderable, except difcovering a large party of the enemy, fuppofed to be near a thoufand, on the eaft-fide of the lake. This party the next day, viz. the 17th, fell upon a detachment of Col. Nicholls's Regiment at the half-way brook, killed three Captains, and upwards of twenty private men.

The 27th another party of the enemy fell upon a convoy of waggoners between Fort Edward and Half-Way Brook, and killed 116 men, fixteen of which were Rangers. In perfuit of this party, with a defign to intercept their retreat, I was ordered to embark the 18th with 700 men; the enemy however efcaped me, and in my return home on the 31ft, I was met by an exprefs from the General, with orders to march with 700 men to South and Eaft Bay, and return by way of Fort Edward, in the profecution of which orders nothing very material happened till the 8th of Auguft; in our return, early in the morning of which day, we decamped from the place where Fort Anne ftood, and began our march, Major Putnam with a party of Provincials marching in the front, my Rangers in the rear, Capt. Dalyell with the regulars in the center, the other officers fuitably difpofed a-

among

mong the men, being in number 530, exclusive of officers (a number having by leave returned home the day before.) After marching about three-quarters of a mile, a fire begun with five hundred of the enemy in the front; I brought my people into as good order as possible, Capt. Dalyell in the center, and the Rangers on the right, with Col. Partridge's light infantry; on the left was Capt. Gidding's of the Boston troops with his people, and Major Putnam being in the front of his men when the fire began, the enemy rushing in, took him, one Lieutenant, and two others, prisoners, and considerably disordered others of the party, who afterwards rallied and did good service, particularly Lieutenant Durkee, who notwithstanding two wounds, one in his thigh, the other in his wrist, kept in the action the whole time, encouraging his men with great earnestness and resolution. Capt. Dalyell with Gage's light infantry, and Lieut. Eyers of the 44th regiment, behaved with great bravery, they being in the center, where was at first the hottest fire, which afterwards fell to the right where the Rangers were, and where the enemy made four different attacks; in short, officers and soldiers throughout the detachment behaved with such vigour and resolution, as in

one

one hour's time broke the enemy, and obliged
them to retreat, which they did with such
caution in small scattering parties, as gave us
no great opportunity to distress them by a pur-
suit; we kept the field and buried our dead.
When the action was over, we had missing
fifty-four men, twenty-one of which afterwards came in, being separated from us while
the action continued. The enemy's loss was
199 killed on the spot, several of which were
Indians *. We arrived at Fort Edward on
the 9th, being met at some distance from it by
Col. Provost, with a party of 300, and re-
freshments for the wounded, which I had desired by an express sent before.

I remained at Fort Edward till the 11th of
the month, when I received orders from Col.
Provost, who now ranked as Brigadier, and
commanded at Fort Edward, to march and
pursue the tracks of a large party of Indians, of
which he had received intelligence, down the
east-side of Hudson's River, in order to secure
our convoys from them, and intercept their
retreat; but this report which the Colonel had
heard being groundless, my scout was ineffec-
tual. I returned to Fort Edward on the 14th,

* By a detachment that went out afterwards, fifty more
of the enemy were found dead near the place of action.

and

and went with my detachment directly to the encampment at Lake George.

Aug. 20, 1758. By orders from the General I embarked with five men in a whale-boat, to visit and reconnoitre Ticonderoga, in which excursion I obtained several articles of intelligence concerning the enemy, their situation and numbers at different posts, and returned the 24th to the encampment at Lake George.

I was employed in various other excursions towards the enemy's forts and frontiers, and in persuit of their flying parties, till the campaign for this year ended, and our army retired to winter-quarters.

Notwithstanding little was effected by our late campaign to Ticonderoga; yet the British arms in America were not every where unsuccessful: for Col. Broadstreet, with a detachment of 2000 men, reduced the French fort at Cataraqua, called Fort Frontenac *, and

---

* This fort was square faced, had four bastions built with stone, and was near three-quarters of a mile in circumferance. Its situation was very beautiful, the banks of the river presenting on every side an agreeable landscape, with a fine prospect of the Lake Ontario, which was distant about a league, interspersed with many islands that were well wooded, and seemingly fruitful. The French had formerly a great trade at this fort with the Indians, it being erected on purpose to prevent their trading with the English; but it is now totally destroyed.

Ge-

General Amherſt, who commanded the Britiſh troops at Cape Breton, had ſucceeded in the reduction of that important fortreſs, and now returned from his conqueſt, with a part of the troops that had been employed there, and was appointed commander in chief of his Majeſty's forces in North America (General Abercrombie embarking for England). The head quarters were now fixed at New York, and I had now new commanders to obey, new companions to converſe with, and, as it were, a new apprenticeſhip to ſerve. From Albany, where I was ſettling ſome accounts with the Paymaſter, I began my acquaintance by the following letter to Col. Townſend, Deputy Adjutant General to his Excellency.

" Sir,   *Albany, Jan.* 28, 1759.

" Incloſed I ſend you the preſent ſtate of his Majeſty's companies of Rangers at Fort Edward, together with a liſt of the officers, now recruiting in the different parts of New England, who have lately adviſed me, that they have already inliſted near 400 men, which recruits are much wanted at Fort Edward, as it

R   may

may be expected that the enemy will soon send their Indians, to endeavour to intercept our convoys between here and Fort Edward.

" To be seasonably strong to prevent their playing their old pranks, I would humbly propose, were it consistent with the service and agreeable to General Amherst, my setting out for New England, in order to dispatch such Rangers as are there with all possible speed to Fort Edward, or otherwise, as his Excellency shall direct. If it should be agreeable to the General that I should go to New England, I should be glad it might be by way of New York, that I might have an opportunity to wait upon the General myself, and represent to him the necessity of an augmentation of the Rangers now at Fort Edward, and the desire of the Stockbridge Indians to re-enter the service.

" The arms of the Rangers are in the hands of Mr. Cunningham at New York, which will be soon wanted at Fort Edward; I should therefore be glad they might be forwarded as soon as may be. I have wrote to Mr. Cunningham, to make application to you for convenient carriages for the same, which I should

be

be glad you would furnish him with. And till the time I have an opportunity of paying you my respects in person, I beg leave to subscribe myself, Sir,

Your most obedient humble servant,

Robert Rogers."

" *P. S.* General Stanwix informs me, that a subaltern officer, and about twenty Rangers, are to be stationed at No. 4; the officer I would recommend for that post, is Lieut. Stephans, who is well acquainted with the country thereabout. He is now recruiting."

To Col. Townsend.

Soon after this I returned to Fort Edward; where I received the Colonel's answer, as follows.

" Sir, *Feb.* 5, 1759.

" I received your letter, with the inclosed return. The General commands me to inform you, he can by no means approve of your leaving Fort Edward.

R 2 " Your

" Your recruiting officers are all ordered to send up their recruits to Fort Edward. They are not only wrote to, but an advertisement is put in all the papers, which was the only method the General had of conveying his intentions to them, as you had not sent me any return of the officers names, and places where they were to recruit at. In obedience to that order, the recruits will be up sooner than if they waited your coming down. I have likewise repeated the order to every officer, according to your return, by this post, and if you are complete by the returns they make, I shall order up every individual officer to their posts.

" Any proposals for the augmentation of the Rangers, or proposals from the Stockbridge Indians, you would chuse to offer to the General, he desires may be immediately sent down to him.

" The arms for the Rangers, which you mention are in the hands of Mr. Cunningham, shall be sent up to you immediately.

" I have wrote to Lieut. Samuel Stephans, to acquaint him with the General's intentions of leaving him at No. 4.

" If

" If the enemy fend out any fcouting parties this year to pick up intelligence, or attack our convoys, the feafon of the year is now coming on that we may expect them; you therefore muft fee the neceffity of your remaining at Fort Edward. Your officers and men fhould join you as faft as poffible. The General would at another time comply with your requeft.

Your obedient humble fervant,

R. *Townfhend*, D. A. G."

Feb. 15, 1759.

To Major Rogers.

I wrote to the Colonel, propofing an addition of two new companies of Rangers, upon the fame footing as thofe already in the fervice, and the raifing of three companies of Indians to ferve the enfuing campaign; and left the Indians fhould be gone out on their hunting parties, and fo be prevented from joining us, I wrote to three of their Sachems, or chiefs; one of which to King Uncus, head Sachem of the Mohegan Indians (which in fubftance is like the

the others) I will here infert, as a fpecimen of
the method in which we are obliged to ad-
drefs thefe favages.

" Brother Uncus,

" As it is for the advantage of his Majefty King
George, to have a large body of Rangers employed in his fervice the enfuing campaign, and
as I am well convinced of the fincere attach-
ment you have to him, I therefore carefully
obey General Amherft's orders to me, to engage your affiftance here early in the fpring.

" I hope you'll continue to fhew that ardent
zeal you have all along expreffed for the Englifh, ever fince you have been allied to them,
by raifing a company of your men with the
utmoft expedition.

" Should you chufe to come out a Captain,
General Amherft will readily give you the
commiffion for it; if not, I fhall expect Do-
quipe and Nunnipad. I leave to you the
choice of an Enfign and two ferjeants; but I
hope you'll engage the fitteft men for their
ftations. I would have the company confift
of fifty private men, or more, if you can get
them; and if thofe men that deferted from
Capt.

Capt. Brewer will join you, the General will pardon them. You may employ a Clerk for the company, to whom General Amherſt will allow the uſual pay.

" I heartily wiſh you ſucceſs in raiſing your men, and ſhall be exceeding glad that you join me with all the expedition you poſſibly can.   I am,

Brother Uncus,

Your moſt obedient humble ſervant,

To King Uncus.   Robert Rogers."

With this letter, or any other wrote to them, in order to give it any credit or influence, muſt go a belt of wampum, ſuitable to the matter and occaſion of it, and upon which the bearer, after having read the letter, interprets it, and then delivers both to the Sachem, or perſon they are directed to.

The latter end of February, about fifty Mohocks, commanded by Captain Lotridge, came from Sir William Johnſon to join me, and proceed to Ticonderoga on a ſcout.

March 3, 1759, I received the following orders from Col. Haldiman : " An officer being choſen

chosen by the General to make observations upon the enemy's situation, and the strength of their forts upon Lake Champlain, you are ordered to march with your Rangers, and the Mohock Indians, under the command of Capt. Lotridge, and take all the measures and precautions possible, that he may execute his intentions, and perform the service, which the General has much at heart; and to effect this with more security, a body of regulars is likewise ordered to join with you, and you are to have the command of the whole. Lieut. Brheem is to communicate his orders to you; and the service being performed, you will endeavour to take a prisoner, or prisoners, or strike such a stroke on the enemy, and try to bring us intelligence.

" He recommends it in the strongest manner, that if some of the enemy should fall into your hands, to prevent the Indians from exercising their. cruelty upon them, as he desires prisoners may be treated with humanity.

Fred. Haldiman,
Commander at
Fort Edward."

Fort Edward,
March 3, 1759.

Pursuant

Purſuant to the above orders, I marched the ſame day with a party of 358 men, officers included, and encamped the firſt night at Half-Way Brook. One Indian, being hurt by accident, returned to Fort Edward. The 4th, marched to within one mile and a half of Lake George, and halted till evening, that we might the better paſs undiſcovered by the enemy, if any were on the hill reconnoitering. We continued our march till two o'clock in the morning, and halted at the firſt narrows. It being exceſſive cold, and ſeveral of our party being froſt-bitten, I ſent back twenty-three, under the charge of a careful ſerjeant, to Fort Edward. We continued here till the evening of the 5th, then marched to Sabbath-day Point; where we arrived about eleven o'clock, almoſt overcome with the cold. At two o'clock we continued our march, and reached the landing-place about eight. I ſent out a ſmall party to obſerve if any of the enemy's parties went out. They returned and reported, that none were to be ſeen on the weſt-ſide of the lake, but on the eaſt were two working parties. It now appeared to be a ſuitable time for the engineer to make his obſervations. I left Capt. Williams to remain at this place with the Regulars, and thirty Rangers, while I, with the engineer,

S   forty

forty-nine Rangers, and Capt. Lotridge, with
forty-five Indians, went to the isthmus that
overlooks the fort, where he made his observations. We returned to our party, leaving five
Indians and one Ranger to observe what numbers crossed the lake in the evening from the
east-side to the fort, that I might know the
better how to attack them next morning. At
dark the engineer went again, with Lieut. Tute,
and a guard of ten men, to the entrenchments,
and returned at midnight without opposition,
having done his business to his satisfaction. On
which I ordered Capt. Williams with the Regulars back to Sabbath-day Point; the party being extremely distressed with the cold, it appeared to me imprudent to march his men
any further, especially as they had no snow-
shoes. I sent with him Lieut. Tute and thirty
Rangers, with directions to kindle fires on the
aforesaid point. At three o'clock I marched with
three Lieutenants and forty Rangers, one Regular, and Capt. Lotridge with forty-six Indians,
in order to be ready to attack the enemy's working parties on the east-side of the lake early in
the morning. We crossed South-Bay about
eight miles south of the fort *; from thence, it

---

* Here we found that a party of Indians had gone up
the bay towards our forts.

being

being about fix o'clock, bore down right oppofite the fort, and within half a mile of where
the French parties, agreeable to our expectations, were cutting of wood. Here I halted,
and fent two Indians and two Rangers to obferve their fituation. They returned in a few
minutes, and brought intelligence, that the
working parties were clofe to the banks of the
lake, and oppofite the fort, and were about forty in number; upon which we ftripped off eur
blankets, and ran down upon them, took feveral prifoners, and deftroyed moft of the party
as they were retreating to the fort, from
whence being difcovered, about eighty Canadians and Indians purfued us clofely, being
backed by about 150 French regulars, and in
a mile's march they began a fire in our rear;
and as we marched in a line abreaft, our front
was eafily made; I halted on a rifing ground,
refolving to make a ftand againft the enemy,
who appeared at firft very refolute: but we repulfed them before their reinforcement came
up, and began our march again in a line abreaft;
having advanced about half a mile further,
they came in fight again. As foon as we
could obtain an advantageous poft, which was
a long ridge, we again made a ftand on the
fide oppofite the enemy. The Canadians and

Indians

Indians came very clofe, but were foon ftopped by a warm fire from the Rangers and Mohocks. They broke immediately, and the Mohocks with fome Rangers purfued, and entirely routed them before their Regulars could come up. After this we marched without any oppofition. In thefe feveral fkirmifhes we had two Rangers and one Regular killed, and one Indian wounded, and killed about thirty of the enemy. We continued our march till twelve o'clock at night, and came to Capt. Williams at Sabbath-day Point (fifty miles diftant from the place we fet out from in the morning.) The Captain received us with good fires, than which fcarce any thing could be more acceptable to my party, feveral of which had their feet froze, it being exceffive cold, and the fnow four feet deep. Next morning marched the whole detachment as far as Long Ifland in Lake George, and there encamped that night. On our march from Sabbath-day Point to this ifland, I gave leave to fome of the Rangers and Indians to hunt near the fide of the lake, who brought us in great plenty of venifon for our refrefhment.

I fent Lieut. Tute, with the following letter, to Col. Haldiman, fearing left a party of Indians we had fome notice of might have

gone

gone up South Bay, and get an opportunity of doing mischief before I could reach Fort Edward with the whole detachmant.

Camp at Sabbath-day Point, Friday, eight o'clock in the morning.

" Sir,

" I send this to let you know that sixty Indians, in two parties, are gone towards Fort Edward and Saratoga, and I fear will strike some blow before this reaches you. Mr. Brheem is satisfied he has done his business agreeable to his orders; since which I have taken some prisoners from Ticonderoga, and destroyed others of the enemy, of the particulars of which the bearer will inform you.

" The Mohocks behaved with great bravery ; some have been within pistol-shot of the French fort.

" Two-thirds of my detachment have froze their feet (the weather being so severe, that it is almost impossible to describe it) some of which we are obliged to carry. I am, &c.

R. Rogers."

Fort

Fort Edward, March 10, 1759.

" Dear Sir,

" I congratulate you heartily on your good ſucceſs, and ſend you twenty-two ſleys to tranſport your ſick. You will, by this opportunity, take as many boards as you can conveniently *. My beſt compliments to Capt. Williams, and to all the gentlemen. I am, Sir,

Your moſt humble ſervant,

Fred. Haldimand.

" *P. S.* I had the ſignal-guns fired to give notice to the different poſts. Nothing has appeared as yet †."

We were met by the ſleys, and a detachment of 100 men at Lake George, and all arrived ſafe at Fort Edward, where I received the following letters upon my arrival.

* Boards left at the place where Fort William-Henry ſtood, and now wanted at Fort Edward.

† The exploſion of theſe ſignal-guns (as we afterwards heard) was heard by the party of the enemy, then near Fort Millar, eight miles below Fort Edward, who thereupon ſuppoſing themſelves diſcovered, retreated with precipitation.

" Sir,

" Sir,

" I yesterday received your letter by Mr. Stark. The General approves of raising the Indian companies; but as he has not heard the Rangers are complete, he cannot agree to the raising more companies, till the present ones are complete at Fort Edward. Mr. Stark sets out to-morrow for New England. I have ordered him to hurry up the recruits of your corps, and repeat my orders to the officers, to join their companies if they are complete. Your arms have been tried and proved by the artillery; they answer very well, and are ordered to be sent to you as fast as possible: the General has sent to you by Capt. Jacobs. We have chose out one hundred men from each regiment, and pitched upon the officers to act this year as light infantry; they are cloathed and accoutred as light as possible, and, in my opinion, are a kind of troops that has been much wanted in this country. They have what ammunition they want, so that I don't doubt but they will be excellent markfmen. You may depend upon General Amherst's intentions to have you; I heard Brigadier Gage mention you to him. From what knowledge I have of the General, I can only say that merit is sure to be rewarded;

rewarded ; nor does he favour any recommendation, without the perfon recommended really
deferves his promotion. You will return your
companies to me as foon as complete.

Your obedient humble fervant,

New York,   *R. Townfhend."*
Feb. 26, 1759.
To Major Rogers.

     " SIR,   *New York, Feb.* 13, 1759.

" This will be delivered to you by Capt. Jacob Nawnawampeteoonk, who laft campaign
commanded a company of Stockbridge Indians,
and who, upon hearing that you had wrote to
me concerning him, came to offer me his fervice for the enfuing campaign: But as you have
not mentioned to me the terms and conditions
on which he was to engage, I have referred
him to you to give in his propofals, that you
may report to me thereupon, and inform me if
you think his fervice adequate to them ; after
which I fhall give you my anfwer. I am, Sir,

Your very humble fervant,

Jeff. Amherft."

To Major Rogers.

Be-

Before I received this letter from his Excellency, I had wrote to him, recommending several officers to the vacancies in the ranging companies, and inclofed a journal of my late fcout; foon after my return from which I went to Albany, to fettle my accompts with the government, where I waited upon his Excellency the General, by whom I was very kindly received, and affured that I fhould have the rank of Major in the army from the date of my commiffion under General Abercrombie.

I returned to Fort Edward the fifteenth of May, where 1 received the melancholy news, that Capt. Burbank, with a party of thirty men, had in my abfence been fent out on a fcout, and were all cut off. This gave me great uneafinefs, as Mr. Burbank was a gentleman I very highly efteemed, and one of the beft officers among the Rangers, and more efpecially as I judged the fcout he was fent out upon by the commanding officer at the fort was needlefs, and unadvifedly undertaken.

Preparations for the campaign were haftened by his Excellency the General in every quarter; the levies from the feveral provinces forwarded, the companies of Rangers compleated, and difciplined in the beft manner I was capable

T   of,

of, and of which the General was pleafed greatly to approve.

In the month of June, part of the army marched with General Gage for the lake. I was ordered to fend three companies there with Capt. Stark, and to remain with the General myfelf with the other three companies, till fuch time as he marched thither. In this interval, purfuant to his Excellency's orders, I fent out feveral parties to the French forts, who from time to time difcovered the fituation of the enemy, and brought fatisfactory intelligence.

About the 20th of June, the General with the remainder of the army marched to the lake, the Rangers being in the advanced guard; and here his Excellency was pleafed to fulfil his promife to me, by declaring in public orders, my rank of Major in the army, from the date of my commiffion, as Major of the Rangers. We continued here collecting our ftrength together, and making neceffary preparations, and getting what intelligence we could of the ftrength and fituation of the enemy, till July 21, 1759, when the army embarked for Ticonderoga. I was in the front with the Rangers on the right wing, and was the firft body that landed on July 22, at the north-end of
Lake

Lake George, followed by the grenadiers and light infantry, which Col. Haviland commanded.

I marched, agreeable to orders from the General, across the mountains in the isthmus; from thence, in a by-way, athwart the woods to the bridge at the Saw-mills; where finding the bridge standing, I immediately crossed it with my Rangers, and took possession of the rising ground on the other side, and beat from thence a party of the enemy, and took several prisoners, killed others, and put the remainder to flight, before Col. Haviland with his grenadiers and light infantry got over. The army took possession that night of the heights near the Saw-mills, where they lay all this evening.

The enemy kept out a scouting-party, with a body of Canadians and Indians, which killed several of our men, and galled us prodigiously.

July 23, the General, early in the morning, put the army in motion; at the same time ordered me in the front, with directions to proceed across the Chesnut Plain, the nighest and best way I could, to Lake Champlain, and do my endeavour to strike it near the edge of the cleared ground, between that and the breastwork, where I was to halt till I received further
orders,

orders. Having purſued my orders, and halted at the lake, I informed the General of my ſituation, and that nothing extraordinary had happened in our march.

The General by this time had appointed and formed a detachment to attack their main breaſt-work on the hill, and had got poſſeſſion of it. I was ordered to ſend two hundred men to take poſſeſſion of a ſmall entrenchment next to Lake Champlain ; and Captain Brewer, whom I had ſent to take poſſeſſion of this poſt, happily ſucceeded.

From the time the army came in ſight the enemy kept up a conſtant fire of cannon from their walls and batteries at our people. The General at this time had left ſeveral Provincial regiments to bring the cannon and ammunition acroſs the Carrying Place, together with proviſions, which they did with great expedition *.

July 24. All this day the engineers were employed in raiſing batteries, as was likewiſe a great part of the army in that work, and in making and fetching faſcines, till the 26th at night; all which time I had parties out to Crown Point to watch the motions of the

---

* About this time ſome of the Provincial regiments were ſent to Oſwego, to aſſiſt in building a fort there.

enemy

enemy there; by which means the General had not only daily, but hourly intelligence from those posts.

I this day received orders from the General to attempt to cut away a boom which the French had thrown across the lake opposite the fort, which prevented our boats from passing by, and cutting off their retreat. For the completion of this order I had sixty Rangers in one English flat-bottomed boat, and two whale-boats *, in which, after night came on, I embarked, and passed over to the other side of Lake Champlain, opposite to the Rangers encampment, and from that intended to steer my course along the east-shore, and privately saw off their boom, for which end I had taken saws with me, the boom being made with logs of timber.

About nine o'clock, when I had got about half way from the place where I had embarked, the enemy, who had undermined their fort, sprung their mines, which blew up with a loud explosion, the enemy being all ready to embark on board their boats, and make a

---

* These boats were carried across the land from Lake George to Lake Champlain, on which day the brave and worthy Col. Townshend was killed by a cannon ball from the enemy, whose fall was much lamented by the General.

retreat.

retreat. This gave me an opportunity to attack them with such success as to drive several of them ashore; so that next morning we took from the east-shore ten boats, with a considerable quantity of baggage, and upwards of fifty barrels of powder, and large quantities of ball. About ten o'clock I returned, and made my report to the General.

The 27th I was ordered with my party to the Saw-mills (to wait the flying parties of the enemy which were expected that way) where I lay till the 11th of August *, on which day I received the following orders from General Amherst.

" SIR,

" You are this night to send a Captain, with a proper proportion of subalterns, and two hundred men, to Crown Point, where the officer is to post himself in such a manner as not to be surprised, and to seize on the best ground for defending himself; and if he should be attacked by the enemy, he is not to retreat

---

* About this time a party of my people discovered that the enemy's Fort at Crown Point was likewise blown up, and the enemy fled.

with

with his party, but keep his ground till he is reinforced from the army. I am, Sir,

Your moſt obedient,

To *Major* Rogers.   *Jeff. Amberſt.*"

Capt. Brewer went with a party, and the General followed the 12th with the whole army, and the ſame day arrived at Crown Point, where it was found that Capt. Brewer had executed his orders extremely well.

This evening I had orders for encamping, and the ground for each corps being laid out, my camp was fixed in the front of the army. Immediately after the General had got the diſpoſition of his camp ſettled, he began to clear ground, and prepare a place for erecting a new fort, in which ſervice great part of the army was employed. I had orders to ſend Capt. Stark, with two hundred Rangers, to cut a road to No. 4. which party was immediately ſent.

During theſe tranſactions I ſent out (by the General's approbation) ſeveral ſcouting parties againſt the enemy *, which brought in pri-

* Capt. Tute, and Lieutenant Fletcher, in two different ſcouting parties, were taken and carried to Canada.

foners from St. John's Fort, and others pe-
netrated into the back country, the better to
learn the nature and fituation of it.

Thus were we employed till the 12th of
September, when the General, exafperated at
the treatment which Capt. Kennedy had met
with, who had been fent with a party as a
flag of truce to the St. Francis Indians, with
propofals of peace to them, and was by them
made a prifoner with his whole party; this
ungenerous inhumane treatement determined
the General to chaftize thefe favages with fome
feverity, and, in order to it, I received from
him the following orders, viz.

* " You are this night to fet out with the
detachment as ordered yefterday, viz. of 200
men, which you will take under your command, and proceed to Mififquey Bay, from
whence you will march and attack the enemy's
fettlements on the fouth-fide of the river St.
Lawrence, in fuch a manner as you fhall judge
moft effectual to difgrace the enemy, and for

* That this expedition might be carried on with the
utmoft fecrefy after the plan of it was concerted the day
before my march, it was put into public orders, that I
was to march a different way, at the fame time I had private
inftructions to proceed directly to St. Francis.

the

the ſucceſs and honour of his Majeſty's arms.

" Remember the barbarities that have been committed by the enemy's Indian ſcoundrels on every occaſion, where they had an opportunity of ſhewing their infamous cruelties on the King's ſubjects, which they have done without mercy. Take your revenge, but don't forget that tho' thoſe villains have daſtardly and promiſcuouſly murdered the women and children of all ages, it is my orders that no women or children are killed or hurt.

" When you have executed your intended ſervice, you will return with your detachment to camp, or to join me wherever the army may be.

Your's, &c.

Camp at Crown Point,   *Jeff. Amherſt.'*
Sept. 13, 1759.

To Major Rogers.

In purſuance of the above orders, I ſet out the ſame evening with a detachment; and as to the particulars of my proceedings, and the great difficulties we met with in effecting our deſign, the reader is referred to the letter I

U

wrote

wrote to General Amherst upon my return, and the remarks following it.

Copy of my Letter to the General upon my return from St. Francis.

" Sir,

" The twenty-second day after my departure from Crown Point, I came in sight of the Indian town St. Francis in the evening, which I discovered from a tree that I climbed, at about three miles distance. Here I halted my party, which now consisted of 142 men, officers included, being reduced to that number by the unhappy accident which befel Capt. Williams*, and several since tiring, whom I was obliged to send back. At eight o'clock this evening I left the detachment, and took with me Lieut. Turner and Ensign Avery, and went to reconnoitre the town, which I did to my satisfaction, and found the Indians in a high frolic or dance. I returned to my party at two

---

* Capt. Williams of the Royal Regiment was, the fifth day of our march, accidentally burnt with gun-powder, and several men hurt, which, together with some sick, returned back to Crown Point, to the number of forty, under the care of Capt. Williams, who returned with great reluctance.

o'clock,

o'clock, and at three marched it to within five hundred yards of the town, where I lightened the men of their packs, and formed them for the attack.

" At half an hour before fun-rife I furprifed the town when they were all faft afleep, on the right, left, and center, which was done with fo much alacrity by both the officers and men, that the enemy had not time to re-cover themfelves, or take arms for their own defence, till they were chiefly deftroyed, ex-cept fome few of them who took to the water. About forty of my people purfued them, who deftroyed fuch as attempted to make their ef-cape that way, and funk both them and their boats. A little after fun-rife I fet fire to all their houfes, except three, in which there was corn, that I referved for the ufe of the party.

" The fire confumed many of the Indians who had concealed themfelves in the cellars and lofts of their houfes. About feven o'clock in the morning the affair was completely over, in which time we had killid at leaft two hun-dred Indians, and taken twenty of their women and children prifoners, fifteen of whom I let go their own way, and five I brought with me, viz. two Indian boys, and three Indian girls.

U 2   I like-

I likewife retoo five Englifh captives, which I alfo took under my care.

" When I had paraded my detachment, I found I had Capt. Ogden badly wounded in his body, but not fo as to hinder him from doing his duty. I had alfo fix men flightly wounded, and one Stockbridge Indian killed.

" I ordered my people to take corn out of the referved houfes for their fubfiftence home, there being no other provifion there; and whilft they were loading themfelves I examined the prifoners and captives, who gave the following intelligence : " That a party of 300 French, and fome Indians, were about four miles down the river below us; and that our boats were way-laid, which I had reafon to believe was true, as they told the exact number, and the place where I left them at: that a party of 200 French and fifteen Indians had, three days before I attacked the town, gone up the river Wigwam Martinic, fuppofing that was the place I intended to attack;" whereupon I called the officers together, to confult the fafety of our return, who were of opinion there was no other way for us to return with fafety, but by No. 4. on Connecticut River. I marched the detachment eight days in a body that way; and when provifions grew fcarce, near Ampara Magog Lake, I divided the detachment into small companies, putting proper guides to each, who were to assemble at the mouth of Amonsook River *, as I expected provisions would be brought there for our relief †, not knowing which way I should return.

" Two days after we parted, Ensign Avery, of Fitche's, fell in on my track, and followed in my rear; and a party of the enemy came upon them, and took seven of his party prisoners, two of whom that night made their escape, and came in to me next morning. Avery, with the remainder of his party, joined mine, and came with me to the Cohase Intervales, where I left them with Lieut. Grant, from which place I, with Capt. Ogden, and one man more, put down the river on a small raft to this place, where I arrived yesterday; and in half an hour after my arrival dispatched provisions up the river to Lieut. Grant in a canoe, which I am pretty certain

* Amonsook River falls into Connectut River about sixty miles above No. 4.

† An officer, upon some intelligence that I had when going out, was sent back to Crown Point from Misisquey Bay, to desire that provisions might be conveyed to this place, as I had reason to believe we should be deprived of our boats, and consequently be obliged to return this way.

will

will reach him this night, and next morning fent two other canoes up the river for the relief of the other parties, loaded with provifions, to the mouth of Amonfook River.

" I fhall fet off to go up the river myfelf to-morrow, to feek and bring in as many of our men as I can find, and expect to be back in about eight days, when I fhall, with all expedition, return to Crown Point. As to other particulars relative to this fcout, which your Excellency may think proper to inquire after, I refer you to Capt. Ogden, who bears this, and has accompanied me all the time I have been out, behaving very well. I am, Sir, with the greateft refpect,

Your Excellency's moft obedient fervant,

No. 4.   R. Rogers."

Nov. 5, 1759.

To General Amherft.

I cannot forbear here making fome remarks on the difficulties and diftreffes which attended us, in effecting this enterprize upon St. Francis, which is fituated within three miles of the river St. Lawrence, in the middle of Canada,

da, about half way between Montreal and
Quebec. It hath already been mentioned, how
our party was reduced by the accident which
befell Capt. Williams, the fifth day after our
departure, and still farther by numbers tiring
and falling sick afterwards. It was extremely
difficult while we kept the water (and which
retarded our progress very much) to pass undiscovered by the enemy, who were then
cruizing in great numbers upon the lake; and
had prepared certain vessels, on purpose to decoy any party of ours, that might come that
way, armed with all manner of machines and
implements for their destruction; but we happily escaped their snares of this kind, and
landed (as hath been mentioned) the tenth
day at Misisquey Bay. Here, that I might
with more certainty know whether my boats
(with which I left provision sufficient to
carry us back to Crown Point) were discovered by the enemy, I left two trusty Indians to
lie at a distance in sight of the boats, and
there to stay till I came back, except the enemy found them; in which latter case they were
with all possible speed to follow on my track,
and give me intelligence. It happened the
second day after I left them, that these two Indians came up to me in the evening, and informed

formed me that about 400 French had difcovered and taken my boats, and that about one
half of them were hotly purfuing on my track.
This unlucky circumftance (it may well be
fuppofed) put us into fome confternation.
Should the enemy overtake us, and we get
the better of them in an encounter; yet being
fo far advanced into their country, where no
reinforcement could poffibly relieve us, and
where they could be fupported by any numbers they pleafed, afforded us little hopes of
efcaping their hands. Our boats being taken,
cut off all hope of a retreat by them; befides,
the lofs of our provifions left with them, of
which we knew we fhould have great need at
any rate, in cafe we furvived, was a melancholy
confideration. It was, however, refolved to
profecute our defign at all adventures, and,
when we had accomplifhed it, to attempt a
retreat (the only poffible way we could think
of) by way of No. 4; and that we might not
be deftroyed by famine in our return, I difpatched Lieut. M'Mullen by land to Crown
Point, to defire of the General to relieve me
with provifion at Amonfook River, at the end
of Cohafe Intervales on Connecticut River, that
being the way I fhould return, if at all, and
the place appointed being about fixty miles
from

from No. 4, then the moſt northerly Engliſh ſettlement. This being done, we determined if poſſible to outmarch our purſuers, and effect our deſign upon St. Francis before they could overtake us. We marched nine days through wet ſunken ground; the water moſt of the way near a foot deep, it being a ſpruce bog. When we encamped at night, we had no way to ſecure ourſelves from the water, but by cutting the bows of trees, and with them erecting a kind of hammocks. We commonly began our march a little before day, and continued it till after dark at night.

The tenth day after leaving Miſiſquey Bay, we came to a river about fifteen miles above the town of St. Francis to the ſouth of it; and the town being on the oppoſite or eaſt ſide of it, we were obliged to ford it, which was attended with no ſmall difficulty, the water being five feet deep, and the current ſwift. I put the talleſt men up ſtream, and then holding by each other, we got over with the loſs of ſeveral of our guns, ſome of which we recovered by diving to the bottom for them. We had now good dry ground to march upon, and diſcovered and deſtroyed the town as before related, which in all probability would have been effected with the loſs of no man but the Indian

X   who

who was killed in the action, had not my
boats been discovered, and our retreat that way
cut off.

This nation of Indians was notoriously at-
tached to the French, and had for near a
century past harrassed the frontiers of New
England, killing people of all ages and sexes
in a most barbarous manner, at a time when
they did not in the least suspect them ; and to
my own knowledge, in six years time, carried into captivity, and killed, on the before mentioned
frontiers, 400 persons. We found in the town
hanging on poles over their doors, &c. about
600 scalps, mostly English.

The circumstances of our return are chiefly
related in the preceding letter ; however, it is
hardly possible to describe the grief and consternation of those of us who came to Cohase
Intervales. Upon our arrival there (after so
many days tedious march over steep rocky
mountains, or thro' wet dirty swamps, with
the terrible attendants of fatigue and hunger)
to find that here was no relief for us, where
we had encouraged ourselves that we should
find it, and have our distresses alleviated ;
for notwithstanding the officer I dispatched to
the General discharged his trust with great
expedition, and in nine days arrived at Crown
Point,

Point, which was an hundred miles thro' the woods, and the General, without delay, sent Lieut. Stephans to No. 4. with orders to take provisions up the river to the place I had appointed, and there wait as long as there was any hopes of my returning; yet the officer that was sent being an indolent fellow, tarried at the place but two days, when he returned, taking all the provisions back with him, about two hours before our arrival. Finding a fresh fire burning in his camp, I fired guns to bring him back, which guns he heard, but would not return, supposing we were an enemy *.

Our distress upon this occasion was truly inexpressible; our spirits, greatly depressed by the hunger and fatigues we had already suffered, now almost entirely sunk within us, seeing no resource left, nor any reasonable ground to hope that we should escape a most miserable death by famine. At length I came to a resolution to push as fast as possible towards No. 4. leaving the remains of my party, now unable

---

* This Gentleman, for this piece of conduct, was broke by a general court-martial, and rendered incapable of sustaining any office in his Majesty's service for the future : a poor reward, however, for the distresses and anguish thereby occasioned to so many brave men, to some of which it proved fatal, they actually dying with hunger.

to

to march further, to get such wretched sub-
sistence as the barren wilderness could afford *,
till I could get relief to them, which I engaged
to do within ten days. I, with Capt. Ogden,
one Ranger, and a captive Indian boy, embarked upon a raft we had made of dry pine-
trees. The current carried us down the
stream in the middle of the river, where we
endeavoured to keep our wretched vessel by
such paddles as we had made out of small
trees, or spires split and hewed. The second
day we reached White River Falls, and very
narrowly escaped being carried over them by
the current. Our little remains of strength
however enabled us to land, and to march by
them. At the bottom of these falls, while
Capt. Ogden and the Ranger hunted for red
squirrels for a refreshment, who had the good
fortune likewise to kill a partridge, I attempted
the forming a new raft for our further con-
veyance. Being not able to cut down trees,
I burnt them down, and then burnt them off
at proper lengths. This was our third day's
work after leaving our companions. The next

---

* This was ground-nuts and lilly roots, which being
cleaned and boiled will serve to preserve life, and the use
and method of preparing which I taught to Lieut. Grant,
commander of the party.

day

day we got our materials together, and
compleated our raft, and floated with the
ſtream again till we came to Wattockquitchey
Falls, which are about fifty yards in length:
here we landed, and by a weath made of ha-
zel buſhes, Capt. Ogden held the raft, till I
went to the bottom, prepared to ſwim in and
board it when it came down, and if poſſible
paddle it aſhore, this being our only reſource
for life, as we were not able to make a third
raft in caſe we had loſt this. I had the good
fortune to ſucceed, and the next morning we
embarked, and floated down the ſtream to
within a ſmall diſtance of No. 4. where we
found ſome men cutting of timber, who gave
us the firſt relief, and aſſiſted us to the fort, from
whence I diſpatched a canoe with proviſions,
which reached the men at Cohaſe four days
after, which (agreeable to my engagement)
was the tenth after I left them.

Two days after my arrival at No. 4. I went
with other canoes, loaded with proviſions,
up the river myſelf, for the relief of others of
my party that might be coming in that way *,

having

---

* I met ſeveral different parties; as Lieut. Curgill, Lieut.
Campbell, Lieut. Farrington, and Serjeant Evans, with their
reſpective diviſions, and ſent canoes further up for the relief

of

having hired some of the inhabitants to assist me in this affair. I likewise sent expresses to Suncook and Pennecook upon Merrimack River, that any who should chance to straggle that way might be assisted; and provisions were sent up said rivers accordingly.

On my return to No. 4. I waited a few days to refresh such of my party as I had been able to collect together, and during my stay there received the following letter from General Amherst, in answer to mine of Nov. 5.

" SIR,   *Crown Point, Nov.* 8, 1759.

" Captain Ogden delivered me your letter of the 5th instant, for which I am not only to thank you, but to assure you of the satisfaction I had on reading it; as every step you inform me you have taken, has been very well judged, and deserves my full approbation. I am sorry Lieut. Stephans judged so ill in coming away with the provisions from the place where I sent him to wait for you.

of such as might be still behind, and coming this way. Some I met who escaped from Dunbar's and Turner's party, who were overtaken (being upwards of twenty in number) and were mostly killed or taken by the enemy.

" An

" An Indian is come in laft night, and faid
he had left fome of your party at Otter River.
I fent for them; they are come in. This afternoon four Indians, two Rangers, a German
woman, and three other prifoners; they quitted four of your party fome days fince, and
thought they had arrived here *. I am in
hopes all the reft will get in very fafe. I think
there is no danger but they will, as you quitted them not till having marched eight days in
a body; the only rifk after that will be
meeting hunting parties. I am, Sir,

Your humble fervant,

To Major Rogers. *Jeff. Amherft.*"

As foon as my party were refrefhed, fuch as
were able I marched to Crown Point, where
I arrived Dec. 1, 1759, and upon examination
found, that, fince our leaving the ruins of St.
Francis, I had loft three officers, viz. Lieut.
Dunbar of Gage's Light Infantry, Lieut. Tur-
ner of the Rangers, and Lieut. Jenkins of the
Provincials, and forty-fix ferjeants and privates.

* Upon our feparation, fome of the divifions were ordered to make for Crown Point, that being the beft route for
hunting.

The

The Rangers at that place were all difmiffed before my return, excepting two companies, commanded by Captains Johnfon and Tute *, with whom I found orders left by the General for me to continue at that garrifon during the winter, but had leave, however, to go down the country, and to wait upon his Excellency at New York.

After giving in my return to the General, and what intelligence I could of the enemy's fituation, he defired me, when I had leifure, to draw a plan of my march to St. Francis; and then, by his order, I returned by the way of Albany; which place I left the 6th of February 1760, with thirteen recruits I had inlifted; and the 13th, on my way between Ticonderoga and Crown Point, my party was attacked by about fixty Indians, who killed five, and took four prifoners. I, with the remainder, made my efcape to Crown Point, from whence I would have purfued them immediately; but Col. Haviland, the commanding officer there, judged it not prudent, by reafon the garrifon at

---

* Capt. Tute, who had been taken prifoner, was returned by a flag of truce, while I was gone to St. Francis.

that

that time was very fickly *. I continued at Crown Point the remainder of the winter.

On the 31ft of March, Capt. James Tute, with two regular officers and fix men, went out a fcouting, and were all made prifoners; the enemy was not purfued, on account of the ficknefs of the garrifon.

The fame day I received from General Amherft the following letter.

" Sir, *New York, March 1, 1760.*

" The command I have received from his Majefty, to purfue the war in this country, has determined me, if poffible, to complete the companies of Rangers that were on foot laft campaign; and as Capt. Wait called upon me yefterday, and reprefented that he could eafily complete the one he commands in the colony of Connecticut and the Province of the Maffachufet's Bay, I have furnifhed him with beating orders for that purpofe, as alfo with a warrant for 800 dollars on account of that fervice.

---

* My own fley was taken with 1196 l. York currency in cafh, befides ftores and other neceffaries; 800 l. of this money belonged to the crown, which was afterwards allowed me, the remaining 396 l. was my own, which I entirely loft.

Y   " This

" This day I have wrote to Capt. John Stark
in New Hampſhire, and Capt. David Brewer
in the Maſſachuſet's Bay, incloſing to each of
them a beating order for the reſpective provinces; and I herewith ſend you a copy of the
inſtructions that accompany the ſame, by
which you will ſee they are ordered, as faſt as
they get any number of men, to ſend them to
Albany. I am, Sir,

Your humble ſervant,

To Major Rogers.   *Jeff. Amherſt.*"

My anſwer to the above.

"Sir,   *Crown Point, March* 15, 1760.

" I received your Excellency's letter, dated
the 1ſt inſtant, together with a copy of your
inſtructions to Capt. John Stark and Capt.
David Brewer, whereby I learn that they are to
be at Albany by the 1ſt of May next with
their companies. Since I received intelligence
from your Excellency that the Rangers are to
be raiſed again, I have wrote to ſeveral of my
friends in New England, who will aſſiſt them
in compleating their companies; and as many
of

of the men belonging to the two companies here were froft-bitten in the winter, and others fick, many of whom I judged would not be fit for fervice the enfuing campaign, I employed Lieut. M'Cormack, of Capt. William Stark's company (that was with Major Scott) Lieut. John Fletcher, and one Holmes, and fent them recruiting the 20th of February for my own and Captain Johnfon's company, and advanced them 1100 dollars. Thefe three recruiters I do not doubt will bring good men enough to complete us here; fo that thofe who are froft-bitten may be fent to hofpitals, and thofe unfit for duty difcharged, or otherwife difpofed of, as your Excellency fhall direct.

There being fo few Rangers fit for duty here, and thofe that are much wanted at this place, has prevented me from propofing any tour to the French and Indian fettlements in purfuit of a prifoner, which may, I believe, be eafily got at any time, if fent for. I am, SIR,

Your Excellency's

moft obedient humble fervant,

. . R. Rogers."

To General Amherft.

A let-

A letter from General Amherſt,

" SIR,   *New York*, 9th *March* 1760.

" As I have not heard that either of the Jacobuſes, who each commanded a company of Stockbridge Indians the laſt campaign, are returned from their captivity; I would have you write (if you think Lieut. Solomon capable of and fit for ſuch a command) to him, to know if he chuſes to accept of the ſame; but it muſt be upon condition of bringing to the field none but good men, that are well inclined, and that are hale and ſtrong. Whatever number he or any of his friends can raiſe that will anſwer this deſcription, I will readily employ this ſummer, and they ſhall meet with all the encouragment their ſervices ſhall merit. All others that are too old or too young, I ſhall re-ject, nor ſhall I make them any allowance of payment, altho' they ſhould join the army; ſo that, in order to prevent his having any diffe-rence with theſe people, it will behove him to engage none but what ſhall be eſteemed fit for the ſervice; he muſt alſo obſerve to be aſſembled with them at Albany by the 1ſt of May at furtheſt, from which day he and they ſhall be entitled to their pay, that is, for ſo many as ſhall

be

be muftered there, and for no more; he muft likewife take care that every man comes provided with a good firelock, and that they be always ready to march at a moment's warning, wherever they are ordered to, in default of which they fhall forfeit their pay that fhall be due to them at that time. All this you will explain to him particularly, and fo foon as you receive his anfwer, inform me thereof. As an encouragement to enter the fervice upon the foregoing conditions, you may affure him alfo, that if he conforms to them in every refpect, and that he and his men prove ufeful, they fhall be better rewarded than they have yet been.

" Capt. Ogden having folicited me for a company of Rangers, affured me that he could raife and complete a very good one in the Jerfies; I have given him a beating order for that purpofe, and inftructions fimilar to thofe I fent you a copy of in my laft for Captains Stark and Brewer, and have alfo granted him a warrant for five hundred dollars, on account of the bounty-money, to be as ufual ftopped out of the firft warrant for the fubfiftence of that company. I am, Sir,

Your humble fervant,

To Major Rogers.   *Jeff. Amherft.*"

My

My Letter to the General.

Crown Point, 20th *March* 1760.

" Sir,

" I obferve the contents of your Excellency's letter of the 19th, and fhall take particular care to let Lieut. Solomon know every circumftance relative to his being employed the next fummer, and to advife your Excellency as foon as I hear from him. He has already informed me he would be glad to engage with fome Indians.

" Mr. Stuart, the Adjutant of the Rangers, who is at Albany, I have defired to go to Stockbridge, to deliver Solomon his orders, and to explain them properly to him.

" I am heartily glad that your Excellency hath been pleafed to give to Capt. Ogden a company of the Rangers, who, from the good character he bears, I doubt not will anfwer your expectations.

" Inclofed is a fketch of my travels to and from St. Francis. I am, Sir,

Your Excellency's moft humble fervant,

To General Amherft.   *R. Rogers.*"

The

The General's Letter to me.

" SIR, *New York*, 6th *April* 1760.

" I am to own the receipt of your letters of the 15th and 20th ultimo, and to approve what you therein mention to have done for completing your and Capt. Johnson's company; as also your having sent Adjutant Stuart to Stockbridge, to deliver Solomon his orders, and to explain them properly to him. This will avoid all miftakes, and enable you the fooner to inform me of Solomon's intentions, which I fhall be glad to know as foon as poffible.

" I thank you for your fketch of your travels to and from St. Francis, and am, Sir,

Your very humble fervant,

To Major Rogers. *Jeff. Amherst.*"

Soon after this I had the pleafure of informing the General that the Stockbridge Indians determined to enter the fervice this year; but as many of them were out a hunting, that they could not be collected at Albany before the 10th of May; and that the recruits of the ranging

ranging companies began to affemble at Crown Point.

May 4, 1760. This day Serjeant Beverly, who had been taken prifoner, and made his efcape, came in feven days from Montreal to Crown Point. He had lived at the Governor's (Monfieur de Vaudreuil) houfe, and brought the following intelligence, which I immediately tranfmitted to the General, viz.

" That about the 10th of April, the enemy withdrew all their troops from Nut Ifland, excepting 300, which they left there to garrifon the place, under the command of Monfieur Bonville : that the enemy alfo brought from the ifland one half of the ammunition they had there, and half of the cannon : that the enemy had two frigates, one of 36 guns, the other of 20 guns, that lay all winter in the river St. Lawrence, and fome other fmall veffels, fuch as row-galleys, &c. that all the troops of France in Canada went down to Jecorty the 20th of April, except thofe left to garrifon their fort, which was very flenderly done, together with all the militia that could be fpared out of the country, leaving only one man to two females to fow their grain, where they were affembled by Monfieur Levy, their General,

neral, with an intent to retake Quebec * : that ninety fix men of the enemy were drowned going down to Jecorty: that he faw a man who was taken prifoner the 15th of April, belonging to our troops at Quebec: that this man told him our garrifon there was healthy; and that Brigadier General Murray had 4000 men fit for duty in the city, befides a poft of 300 men at Point Levy, which the enemy attempted to take poffeffion of in the month of February laft, with a confiderable body of troops, and began to fortify a church at or near the Point, but that General Murray fent over a detachment of about 1000 men, which drove the enemy from their poft, and took a Captain, with about thirty French foldiers, prifoners, and fortified the church for his own conveniency: that the General has another poft on the north-fide of the river at Laurat, a little diftance from the town, in which he keeps 300 men : that there is a line of blockhoufes well fortified all round the land-fide of the town, under cover of the cannon: that a breaft-work of fraziers is extended from one

* This place, the capital of all Canada, had been taken by the Englifh troops laft year, under the command of General Wolfe.

Z

block-

block-house to another, as far as those houses extend: that they heard at Quebec of the enemy's coming, but were not in the least concerned: that a detachment from Quebec surprised two of the enemy's guards, at a place called Point de Treamble, each guard consisting of fifty men, and killed or took the most part of them. One of those guards were all granadiers."

He moreover reports, " That two more of our frigates had got up the river, and that two more men of war were near the Island of Orleans: that the French told him that there was a fleet of ten sail of men of war seen at Gaspée Bay, with some transports, but put back to sea again on account of the ice; but as they had up different colours, they could not tell whether they were French or English: that the beginning of May the enemy was to draw off 2000 of their men to Nut Island, and as many more to Oswagotchy: he heard that they did not intend to attack Quebec, except the French fleet gets up the river before ours: that 100 Indians were to come this way, and set out about the fifth of May; the remainder of the Indians were at present gone to Jecorty: that Gen. Levy, the Attawawas, and Cold Country Indians, will all be in Canada by the beginning

ning of June, ten Sachems being fent by the
French laft fall, to call thofe nations to their
affiftance : that a great number had deferted
to the French from the battalion of Royal
Americans at Quebec, which the French have
engaged in their fervice; but that they were
to be fent off, under the care of Monfieur Boar-
bier, up to Attawawas River, to the French
colony betwixt the lakes and the Miffiffipi
River : that the moft part of the enemy's Indians are intent on going there ; and that a
great number of French, efpecially thofe who
have money, think to fave it by carrying it to
New Orleans : that he faw at Montreal two
Rangers, Reynolds and Hall, that were returned by Col. Haviland deferted laft fall: that
they were taken prifoners near River-head
Block-houfe, when after cattle : that two
more Rangers are to be here in ten days with
frefh intelligence from Montreal, if they can
poffibly make their efcape : that Monfieur
Longee, the famous partifan, was drowned in
the river St. Laurence, a few days after he returned with the party that took Capt. Tute :
that the Indians have a great eye to the No. 4.
roads, as they fay they can get fheep and oxen
coming here from that place: that he heard Gen.
Murray had hanged feveral Canadians lately,

Z 2   that

that were carrying ammunition out of Quebec
to the enemy : that the two Captains Jacobs
are ftill in Canada ; the one taken with Capt.
Kennedy is on board a veffel in irons, the other
ran away laft fall, but returned, having froze
his feet, and is at Montreal."

A few days after this, I went down the Lake
Champlain, to reconnoitre Nut Ifland, and the
garrifon there, the landing places, &c. On my
return from that fervice to Crown Point, I had
an order from Gen. Amherft to repair to Albany, the head-quarters, as faft as poffible.

I fet out, in obedience to this order, the 18th
of May, and waited upon the General at Albany the 23d, and gave him all the information I could, in regard to the paffage into Canada by the Ifland de Noix, or Nut Ifland,
and likewife that by Ofwego and La Galette.

The General being acquainted by an exprefs,
that Quebec was then befieged by the French,
informed me of his intentions of fending me
with a party into Canada, and if the fiege of
Quebec was continued, to deftroy their country
as far as poffible, and by conftantly marching
from one place to another, try to draw off the
enemy's troops, and prolong the fiege till our
veffels got up the river. He ftrongly recommended, and ordered me to govern myfelf ac-
cor-

cording to the motions of the French army;
to retreat if they had raiſed the ſiege ; and in
caſe, by priſoners or otherwiſe, I ſhould find
the ſiege ſtill going on, to harraſs the country,
tho' it were at the expence of my party. I had
at the ſame time the following inſtructions
from him in writing:

"Major Rogers, you are to take under your
command a party of 300 men, compoſed of
275 Rangers, with their proper officers, and a
ſubaltern, two ſerjeants, and twenty-five men
of the Light Infantry regiments ; with which
detachment you will proceed down the lake,
under convoy of the brig, where you will fix
upon the ſafeſt and beſt place for laying up
your boats, which I imagine one of the iſlands
will beſt anſwer, while you are executing the
following ſervices.

"You will with 250 men land on the weſt-
ſide, in ſuch manner that you may get to St.
John's (without the enemy at the Iſle au Noix
having any intelligence of it) where you will
try to ſurprize the fort, and deſtroy the veſſels,
boats, proviſions, or whatever elſe may be
there for the uſe of the troops at the Iſle au
Noix. You will then march to Fort Cham-
blé, where you will do the ſame, and you will
deſtroy

deſtroy every magazine you can find in that part, ſo as to diſtreſs the enemy as much as you can. This will ſoon be known at the Iſle au Noix, and you muſt take care not to be cut off in your retreat; for which reaſon, when you have done all you think practicable on the weſtern-ſide, I judge your beſt and ſafeſt retreat will be, to croſs the river and march back the eaſt-ſide of Iſle au Noix. When you land on the weſt-ſide, you will ſend ſuch officer with the fifty Rangers, as you think will beſt anſwer their intended ſervice, which is, to march for Wigwam Martinique, to deſtroy what he may find there and on the eaſt ſide of the river, and afterwards to join you, or to retreat in ſuch manner as you will direct him. You will take ſuch proviſions as you judge neceſſary with you, and fix with Capt. Grant (who ſhall have orders to wait for your return) the places where he may look out for you when you come back.

" You will take your men as light with you as poſſible, and give them all the neceſſary caution for the conduct, and their obedience to their officers; no firing without order, no unneceſſary alarms, no retreating without an order; they are to ſtick by one another and nothing can hurt them; let every man whoſe firelock will carry it have a bayonet; you are not
to

to suffer the Indians to destroy women or children, no plunder to be taken to load your men, who shall be rewarded at their return as they deserve.

May 25, 1760.   *Jeff. Amberst.*"

With the above instructions the General delivered me a letter directed to General Murray at Quebec, desiring me to convey it to him in such manner as I thought would be quickest and safest.

Having received these instructions I returned to Crown Point as fast as possible, and about the beginning of June set out from thence with a party of two hundred and fifty men * down Lake Champlain, having four vessels, on board of which this detachment embarked, putting our boats and provisions into them, that the enemy might have less opportunity of discovering our designs.

The 3d, I landed Lieut. Holmes with fifty men in Misisquey Bay, and gave him proper

* The Stockbridge Indians who had been mustered at, and now marched from Albany, and who were to be a part of the detachment of 300, agreeable to the General's orders, had not arrived at Crown Point at the time of my embarkation, but were ordered to follow after and join me.

directions

directions agreeable to my orders from the General, informing him that one of the sloops should cruise for him till his return, which upon signals that were given him would take him on board, upon which he was to join me or wait on board till my return, as the situation of affairs might direct him. Here likewise I sent the letter I had received from the General to Brigadier Murray, thro' the woods, and gave the following instructions to the officer I intrusted with it, viz.

Instructions for Serjeant Beverly of his Majesty's Rangers.

" You are hereby directed to take under your command, these three men, viz. John Shute, Luxford Goodwin, and Joseph Eastman, and march them from Misisquey Bay, to which place you will be convoyed by Lieut. Holmes with a party I have sent there for a particular purpose; you are to land in the night-time, as otherwise you may be discovered by a party from the Isle au Noix; you will steer your course about north-east, and make all the dispatch you possibly can with the letter in your charge to Quebec, or to the English army at or near that place, and deliver it to Brigadier
Murray,

or to the officer commanding his Majefty's
forces in or upon the river St. Lawrence. A
fketch of the country will be delivered you
with thefe orders, that you may the better
know the confiderable rivers you have to crofs,
betwixt Mififquey Bay and Quebec. The dif-
tances are marked in the draught, as is the road
I travelled in laft fall, from Mififquey Bay to
St. Francis, which road you will crofs feveral
times, if you keep the courfe I before directed.
The rivers are fo plainly defcribed in the plan,
that you will know them when you come to
them. The river St. Francis is about half-way
of your journey, and is very ftill water, and
may be eafily rafted where you crofs it; but
lower down it is fo fwift and rapid that you
muft not attempt it. Shedoir River you will
likewife be obliged to pafs on a raft; it is fwift
water for fome miles from its mouth; you had
better examine it well before you attempt to
crofs it. As foon as you pafs this river, fteer
your courfe about eaft, leaving Point Levy on
your left hand, and fall in with the river St.
Lawrence, near the lower end of the ifland of
Orleans, as it may be poffible that Gen. Murray may have encamped the army either at the
ifle of Orleans or the ifle of Quodoa; therefore
you are not to depend on finding at once the

A a
exact

exact place of his encampment, but are posi-
tively ordered to look out for the English fleet,
and the first line of battle ship you see, you
are to venture on board, as I think it not possible the enemy should have any large ships
there, and whatever English ship you get on
board of, will convoy you directly to General
Murray, when you will deliver him the verbal
message I told you. You may apply to the
General for fifty pounds, who will pay it to
you, and also give you proper directions to join
me as soon as you have rested yourself from
your march. I wish you a good journey,
and am,

Your's, &c.

To Serjeant Beverley.   Robert Rogers."

As soon as I had dispatched the two parties
before-mentioned, I, with the remainder,
crossed Lake Champlain to the west-side, and
the 4th in the morning got into my boats, and
landed with about 200 men, about twelve
miles south of the island Noix, with an intent
to put in execution the General's orders to me
of May 5th with all speed. Capt. Grant
sent the two sloops to attend, which I ordered

to

to cruize further down the lake than where I landed, and nearer to their fort, to command the attention of the enemy till I could get into their country. I lay ftill all the 5th, there being a heavy rain, and the bufhes fo wet that both we and our provifions would have been greatly expofed by a march.

In the afternoon of this day, feveral French boats appeared on the Lake, which were difcovered by the two floops, as well as by my party on the fhore. Thefe boats continued as near as they could to our veffels without endangering themfelves, till after dark. Concluding their boats would cruize the whole night to watch the motions of our floops, I imagined it would be a prudent ftep to fend the floops back to Capt. Grant, the commander of thefe veffels, who lay near Mott Ifland; I accordingly went to the floops in a boat after dark, and ordered them to return. The enemy, who kept all night in their boats, having, by a ftrict look-out, difcovered where I landed, fent a detachment from the ifland next morning to cut off my party. I difcovered their intentions by my reconnoitering parties, who counted them as they croffed from the fort in the morning in their boats, to the weft-fhore, and informed me that they were

350 in number. I had intelligence again
when they were about a mile from us. Half
after eleven they attacked me very briskly on
my left, having on my right a bog, which
they did not venture over, thro' which, however, by the edge of the lake, I sent seventy of
my party to get round and attack them in the
rear. This party was commanded by Lieut.
Farrington. As soon as he began his attack,
I pushed them in front, which broke them
immediately. I pursued them with the greatest part of my people about a mile, where they
retired to a thick cedar swamp, and divided
into small parties. By this time it rained again
very hard. I called my party immediately together at the boats, where I found that Ensign
Wood of the 17th regiment was killed, Capt.
Johnson wounded through the body, a second shot thro' his left arm, and a third in his
head. I had two men of the Light Infantry,
and eight Rangers, wounded, and sixteen Rangers killed. We killed forty of the enemy,
and recovered about fifty firelocks. Their
commanding officer, Monsieur la Force, was
mortally hurt, and several of the party were
likewise wounded. After the action I got
the killed and maimed of my detachment
together in battoes, returned with them to the

Isle

Isle à Mot. near which the brig lay. I dispatched one of the vessels to Crown Point, on board of which was put the corpse of Mr. Wood, but Capt. Johnson died on his passage thither); this vessel I ordered to bring more provisions. I buried the rest of the dead on an island, and then began to prepare for a second landing; being joined about this time by the Stockbridge Indian Company, I was determined at all adventures to pursue my orders, settled the plan of landing, and left the following instructions with Capt. Grant, viz.

" You will be so good as to fall down the lake with your vessels as soon as possible, as far as the Wind Mill Point, or near where you lay at anchor the last time I was with you, and cruize near it for two or three days, which will be the only method I can think of that has any appearance of attracting the attention of the enemy till I get into their country; as soon as I observe or think you pretty near the Wind Mill Point, I shall land with my party on the west-side opposite to the north-end of the Isle à Mot, in the river that runs into the bay which forms itself there, and from thence proceed to execute the General's orders. If they do not attack me in my march till I compleat my design, you may be certain

I shall

I shall come back on the east-side, and endeavour to join you near the Wind Mill Point, or betwixt that and the Isle à Mot. When I arrive, the signal that I will make for your discovering me, will be a smoak and three guns, at a minute's interval each from the other, and repeated a second time, in half an hour after the first; but if the enemy should attack me on my march before I get to the place I am ordered, which I believe they will do, in case I am worsted I shall be obliged to come back on the west-side, and shall make the before mentioned signals betwixt the Isle à Mot and the place where I had the battle with the enemy the 6th instant. It is uncertain when I shall be at either shore; so that I would recommend it to you not to come back south of the Isle à Mot till my return, as a contrary wind might prevent your getting in with your vessels to relieve me. I send you Serjeant Hacket and ten Rangers, to be with you in my absence, as we this day agreed. If Lieutenant Darcy comes down in season to go with me, I shall leave Ensign Wilson with you; but if Darcy should not come till after I land, you'll be pleased to take him under your direction, as well as all those that may come with him to join me; tho' I would recommend it not

to

to send any party to the island, to take a prisoner, till the fifth day after my landing, as the loss of a man from us may be of very bad consequence. Lieutenant Holmes has appointed between the eleventh and sixteenth day after his landing for his return to Misisquey Bay, and from the eleventh to the sixteenth, as before mentioned; I should be glad the sloop might cruize for him at the place he is appointed to meet her. I am, Sir,

Your humble servant,

R. Rogers."

I cannot but observe with pleasure, that Mr. Grant, like an able officer, very diligently did all that could be expected of him for the good of the service, carefully attending with his vessels till my return from this second excursion, on which I embarked with two hundred and twenty men, officers included, and landed the 9th of June, about midnight, on the west-shore opposite the Isle à Mot, from thence marched as fast as possible to St. John's, and came to the road that leads from it to Montreal, about two miles from the fort, the evening of the 15th. At eleven o'clock this night, I marched with an an intent to surprise the fort, to within four hundred yards of it, where I halted to reconnoitre; which I did, and found they had more men than I expected. The number of the centries within the fort were seventeen, and so well fixed, that I thought it was impossible for me to take the place by surprise, especially as they had seen me, and fired several guns accordingly. I left it at two o'clock, and marched down the river to St. d'Etrese; at break of day I reconnoitred this place, and found that the enemy had in it a stockaded fort, defensible against small arms. I observed two large store-houses in the inside, and that the enemy were carting hay into the fort. I waited for an opportunity when the cart had just entered the gate-way, run forward, and got into the fort before they could clear the way for shutting the gate. I had at this time sent different parties to the several houses, about fifteen in number, which were near the fort, and were all surprised at the same instant of time, and without firing a single gun. We took in the fort twenty-four soldiers, and in the houses seventy-eight prisoners, women and children included; some young men made their escape to Chamblee. I examined the prisoners, and found I could not

pro-

proceed to Chamblee with any prospect of suc-
cefs; therefore concluded my best way was to
burn the fort and village, which I did, together
with a confiderable magazine of hay, and fome
provifions, with every battoe and canoe, except
eight battoes which I kept to crofs the river,
and thefe we afterwards cut to pieces: we alfo
killed their cattle, horfes, &c. deftroyed their
waggons, and every other thing which we
thought could ever be of fervice to the enemy.
When this was done, I fent back the women
and children, and gave them a pafs to go to
Montreal, directed to the feveral officers of the
different detachments under my command. I
continued my march on the eaft-fide of Lake
Champlain, and when paffing by Mififquey
Bay, oppofite the Ifle Noix, my advance-
party, and the advance-party of about 800
French, that were out after me from their fort,
engaged with each other; but the body of the
enemy, being about a mile behind their advance-
party, retreated, to my great fatisfaction. I
purfued my march with all poffible fpeed: and
the fame day, being the 20th day of June, arrived at the lake oppofite where the veffels lay;
and as I had fent a few men forward to repeat
the fignals, the boats met us at the fhore. We
directly put on board, the enemy foon after appeared

B b

peared on the fhore where we embarked. I had not at this time any account from Lieutenant Holmes, either by prifoners or otherways.

Upon examination the prifoners reported, (fome of them had been at the fiege of Quebec) " that the French loft five hundred men there; and that they retreated after twelve days bombarding and cannonading, and came to Jack's quarters, where General Levy left five hundred men, being compofed of a picquet of each battalion of the army, and that there were four hundred Canadians who ftaid voluntarily with them; that the reft of the army was quartered by two's and three's on the inhabitants, from there to St. John's. In Montreal there are about a hundred and fifty troops, and the inhabitants do duty. That in Chamblee Fort are about one hundred and fifty men, including workmen; and the remnant of the Queen's regiment are in the village. That there are twelve cannon at St. John's, and about three hundred men, including workmen, who are obliged to take arms on any alarm. That at the Ifle au Noix are about eight hundred ftationed, befides the fcouts between that and Montreal. That there are about an hundred pieces of cannon there." This is the fubftance of their report,

in

in which they all agree, and which, with an account of my proceedings, I tranſmitted to the General.

On the 21ſt I put the twenty-ſix priſoners on board one of the veſſels, with fifty men of my detachment, and ordered her to proceed to Crown Point, and tarried with the other veſſels to cover Mr. Holmes's retreat, who joined us the ſame evening, without having ſucceeded in his enterpriſe, miſſing his way by following down a river that falls into Sorrel, inſtead of that called Wigwam Martinic, which empties itſelf into St. Lawrence at Lake St. Francis. I arrived at Crown Point the 23d of June, and encamped my Rangers on the eaſt-ſhore, oppoſite the fort.

The following letter I received from General Amherſt, dated at Canijoharry, June 26, 1760.

" Sir,

" Colonel Haviland ſent me your letter of June 21, which I received laſt night, and ſaw with pleaſure you was returned without the loſs of a man of your party, and that you had done every thing that was prudent for you to attempt with the number of men you had un-

der

der your command. From the fituation the enemy is now in, by being forced back to their former quarters, on Governor Murray's having obliged them to abandon their cannon, and raife the fiege of Quebec, I hope Lieutenant Holmes will return with equal fuccefs as you have done. I am, Sir,

Your humble fervant,

To Major Rogers.   Jeff. Amherft."

I remained at Crown Point with my people, without effecting any thing confiderable, more than in fmall parties reconnoitring the country about the fort, while every thing was got in readinefs for embarking the army the 16th of Auguft; which was done accordingly, having one brig, three floops, and four rideaus, which latter were occupied by the royal train of artillery, commanded by Lieut. Colonel Ord. Our order of march was as follows, viz.

Six hundred Rangers and feventy Indians in whale-boats in the front, commanded by Major Rogers, as an advance-guard for the whole army, all in a line a-breaft, about half a mile a-head of the main body, followed by the light infantry and grenadiers in two columns,

two

two boats a-breaft in each column, commanded
by Col. Darby. The right wing was compofed of Provincials, commanded by Brigadier
Ruggles, who was fecond in command of the
whole army. The left was made up of New
Hampfhire and Bofton troops, commanded by
Col. Thomas. The feventeenth and twenty-
feventh regiments, with fome few of the Roy-
als, that formed the center column, were commanded by Major Campbell of the 17th regiment. Col. Haviland was in the front of thefe
divifions, between that and the light infan-
tery, and grenadiers. The royal artillery followed the columns, and was commanded
by Colonel Ord, who had, for his efcort, one
Rhode Ifland regiment of Provincials. The
futlers, &c. followed the artillery. In this
manner we rowed down the lake forty miles
the firft day, putting afhore where there was
good landing on the weft-fide, and there encamped.

The day following we lay by. The 18th,
the wind blowing frefh at fouth, orders were
given for embarking, and the fame day reached
a place on the weft-fhore, within ten miles of
the Ifle à Mot, where the army encamped. It
having blown a frefh gale moft part of the day,
fome of my boats fplit open by the violence of
the

the waves, and ten of my Rangers were thereby drowned.

The 19th we set sail again early in the morning, and that night encamped on the north-end of the Isle à Mot.

The 20th, before day, the army was under way, with intention to land; having but twenty miles to go, and having the advantage of a fair wind, we soon came in sight of the French fort, and about ten in the morning Col. Darby, with the Grenadiers and Light Infantry, and myself with the Rangers, landed on the east-shore, and marched and took possession of the ground opposite the fort on that side, without the least opposition. Having done this, an officer was sent to acquaint Col. Haviland (who, with the remainder of the army, was at the place where we landed) that there was not the least danger to apprehend from the enemy. The next day we began to raise batteries, and soon after to throw some shells into the garrison. About the 24th a proposal was made for taking the enemy's vessels, three of which were at anchor a little below the fort, and some of their rideaus likewise. It was introduced by Col. Darby, who was ordered to take the command of the party appointed for this service, which consisted of two companies of Regulars, and

four

four companies of my Rangers, with the Indians. We carried with us two light hobitzers
and one fix-pounder, and filently conveying
them along thro' the trees, brought them oppofite the veffels, and began a brifk fire upon
them, before they were in the leaft apprifed of
our defign, and, by good fortune, the firft fhot
from the fix-pounder cut the cable of the great
rideau, and the wind being at weft, blew her
to the eaft-fhore, where we were, and the o-
ther veffels weighed anchor and made for St.
John's, but got all a-ground, in turning a point
about two miles below the fort. I was, by
Col. Darby, ordered down the eaft-fhore with
my Rangers, and croffed a river of about thirty
yards wide, whieh falls into Lake Champlain
from the eaft. I foon got oppofite the veffels,
and, by firing from the fhore, gave an opportunity to fome of my party to fwim on board with
their tomahawks, and took one of the veffels; in
the mean time Col. Darby had got on board the
rideau, and had her manned, and took the other
two; of which fuccefs he immediately acquainted Col. Haviland, who fent down a fufficient
number of men to take charge of and man the
veffels; and ordered the remainder of the Rangers, Light Infantry and Grenadiers, to join the
army that night, which was accordingly done;
and

and about midnight the night following the French troops left the island, and landed safe on the main; so that next morning nothing of them was to be seen but a few sick, and Col. Haviland took possession of the fort.

The second day after the departure of Monsieur Bonville and his troops from the island, Mr. Haviland sent me with my Rangers to pursue him as far as St. John's Fort, which was about twenty miles further down the lake, and at that place I was to wait the coming of the army, but by no means to follow further than that fort, nor run any risk of advancing further towards Montreal. I went in boats, and about day-light got to St. John's, and found it just set on fire. I pursued, and took two prisoners, who reported, " That Monsieur Bonville was to encamp that night about half-way on the road to Montreal; and that he went from St. John's about nine o'clock the night before; but that many of their men were sick, and that they thought some of the troops would not reach the place appointed till the middle of the afternoon." It being now about seven in the morning, I set all hands to work, except proper guards, to fortify the loghouses that stood near the lake-side, in order that part of my people might cover the

the battoes, while I, with the remainder, followed Monſieur Bonville, and about eight o'clock I got ſo well fortified, that I ventured our boats and baggage under the care of 200 Rangers, and took with me 400, together with the two companies of Indians, and followed after the French army, which conſiſted of about 1500 men, and about 100 Indians they had to guard them. I was reſolved to make his dance a little the merrier, and purſued with ſuch haſte, that I overtook his rear-guard about two miles before they got to their encamping ground. I immediately attacked them, who, not being above 200, ſuddenly broke, and then ſtood for the main body, which I very eagerly purſued, but in good order, expecting Monſieur Bonville would have made a ſtand, which however he did not chuſe, but puſhed forward to get to the river, where they were to encamp, and having croſſed it, pulled up the bridge, which put a ſtop to my march, not judging it prudent to croſs at a diſadvantage, inaſmuch as the enemy had a good breaſt-work on the other ſide, of which they took poſſeſſion; in this purſuit, however, we conſiderably leſſened their number, and returned in ſafety.

In the evening Mr. Haviland came in ſight, and landed at St. John's. As ſoon as he came

on

on fhore, I waited upon him, and acquainted him with what I had done, &c. and that I had two prifoners for him; he faid it was very well, and ordered his troops to encamp there that night, and next day went down the river Sorriel, as far as St. d'Etrefe, where he encamped, and made a ftrong breaft-work, to defend his people from being furprifed. I was fent down the river Sorriel, to bring the inhabitants under fubjection to his Britannic Majefty, and went into their fettled country in the night, took all their priefts and militia officers, and fent fome of them for the inhabitants. The firft day I caufed all the inhabitants near Chamblee to take the oaths of allegiance, &c. who appeared glad to have it in their power to take the oaths and keep their poffeffions, and were all extremely fubmiffive. Having obliged them to bring in their arms, and fulfilled my inftructions in the beft manner I could, I joined Col. Darby at Chamblee, who came there to take the fort, and had brought with him fome light cannon. It foon furrendered, as the garrifon confifted only of about fifty men. This happened on the firft of September.

On the 2d, our army having nothing to do, and having good intelligence both from Gen. Amherft and Gen. Murray, Mr. Haviland fent
me

me to join the latter, while he marched with the reſt of the army for La Pierre. The 5th in the morning I got to Longville, about four miles below Montreal, oppoſite to where Brigadier Murray lay, and gave him notice of my arrival, but not till the morning of the 6th, by reaſon of my arriving ſo late.

By the time I came to Longville, the army, under the command of Gen. Amherſt, had landed about two miles from the town, where they encamped ; and early this morning Monſieur de Vaudreuil, the governor and commander in chief of all Canada, ſent out to capitulate with our General, which put a ſtop to all our movements till the 8th of September, when the articles of capitulation were agreed to, and ſigned, and our troops took poſſeſſion of the town-gates that night. Next morning the Light Infantry, and Granadiers of the whole army, under the command of Col. Haldiman, with a company of the royal artillery, with two pieces of cannon, and ſome hobitzers, entered the town, retaking the Engliſh colours belonging to Pepperel's and Shirley's regiments, which had been taken by the French at Oſwego.

Thus, at length, at the end of the fifth campaign, Montreal and the whole country of Canada was given up, and became ſubject to the

King

King of Great Britain; a conqueſt perhaps of the greateſt importance that is to be met with in the Britiſh annals, whether we conſider the prodigious extent of country we are hereby made maſters of, the vaſt addition it muſt make to trade and navigation, or the ſecurity it muſt afford to the northern provinces of America, particularly thoſe flouriſhing ones of New England and New York, the irretrievable loſs France ſuſtains hereby, and the importance it muſt give the Britiſh crown among the ſeveral ſtates of Europe: all this, I ſay, duly conſidered, will, perhaps, in its conſequences render the year 1760 more glorious than any preceding.

And to this acquiſition, had we, during the late war, either by conqueſt or treaty, added the fertile and extenſive country of Louiſiana, we ſhould have been poſſeſſed of perhaps the moſt valuable territory upon the face of the globe, attended with more real advantages than the ſo-much-boaſted mines of Mexico and Peru, and would have for ever deprived the French, thoſe treacherous rivals of Britain's glory, of an opportunity of acting hereafter the ſame perfidious parts they have already ſo often repeated.

On

On the 9th Gen. Amherft informed me of his intention of fending me to Detroit, and on the 12th in the morning, when I waited upon him again, I received the following orders:

By his Excellency Jeffery Amherft, Efq; Major General and Commander in Chief of all his Majefty's forces in North America, &c. &c. &c.

To Major Rogers, commanding his Majefty's independant companies of Rangers.

" You will, upon receipt hereof, wirh Capt. Waite's and Capt. Hazen's companies of Rangers under your command, proceed in whaleboats from hence to Fort William-Auguftus, taking along with you one Jofeph Poupao, alias La Fleur, an inhabitant of Detroit, and Lieut. Brehme, Affiftant Engineer.

" From Fort William-Auguftus you will continue your voyage by the north-fhore to Niagara, where you will land your whale-boats, and tranfport them acrofs the Carrying place into Lake Erie, applying to Major Walters, or the officer commanding at Niagara, for any affiftance you may want on that or any other occafion, requefting of him at the fame time to deliver up

to

to you Monfieur Gamelin, who was made prifoner at the reduction of faid fort, and has continued there ever fince, in order to conduct
him, with the above-mentioned Poupao, to
their habitations at Detroit, where, upon taking the oath of allegiance to his moft facred
Majefty, whofe fubjects they are become by the
capitulation of the 8th inftant; they fhall be
protected in the peacable and quiet poffeffion
of their properties, and, fo long as they behave
as becometh good and faithful fubjects, fhall
partake of all the other privileges and immuni-
ties granted unto them by the faid capitulation.

" With thefe, and the detachment under
your command, you will proceed in your
whale-boats acrofs Lake Erie to Prefque Ifle,
where, upon your arrival, you will make
known the orders I have given to the officer
commanding that poft; and you will leave
faid whale-boats and party, taking only a fmall
detachment of your party, and marching by
land, to join Brigadier General Monkton,
wherever he may be.

" Upon your arrival with him, you will deliver into his hands the difpatches you fhall
herewith receive for him, and follow and obey
fuch orders as he fhall give you for the relief
of

of the garrisons of the French posts at Detroit,
Michlimakana, or any others in that district,
for gathering in the arms of the inhabitants
thereof, and for administering to them the
oath of allegiance already mentioned ; when
you will likewise administer, or see administer-
ed, the same to the before-mentioned Gamelin
and Poupao; and when this is done, and that
you have reconnoitered and explored the country as much as you can, without losing time
unnecessarily, you are to bring away the French
troops and arms, to such place as you shall be
directed by Gen. Monkton.

"And when the whole of this service is
compleated, you will march back your detachment to Presque Isle, or Niagara, according to the
orders you receive from Brigadier Monkton,
where you will embark the whole, and in like
manner, as before, transport your whale-boats
across the Carrying-place, into Lake Ontario,
where you will deliver over your whale-boats
into the care of the commanding officer,
marching your detachment by land to Albany,
or wherever I may be, to receive what further orders I may have to give you.

Given

" Given under my hand, at the head quarters in the camp of Montreal, 12th Sept. 1760.

Jeff. Amherst."

By his Excellency's command,

J. Appy."

An additional order was given, which was to be shewn only to the commanding officers of the different posts I might touch at, the expedition being intended to be kept a profound secret, for fear the march should be impeded by the enemy Indians, through whose country I was obliged to march.

This order was as follows, viz.

" Major Walters, or the officer commanding at Niagara, will judge whether or not there is provision sufficient at Presque Isle ; and Major Rogers will accordingly take provisions from Niagara. Eight days provision will take him from Montreal to Fort William-Augustus ; there he will apply to the commanding officer for a sufficient quantity to proceed to Niagara. Major Rogers knows where he is going, and the provisions he will want ; some should be

in

in ftore likewife at Prefque Ifle, for the party
Brigadier General Monkton will fend.

Jeff. Amherft.

Montreal, 12th Sept. 1760.

In purfuance of thefe orders I embarked at
Montreal the 13th Sept. 1760 (with Captain
Brewer, Captain Wait, Lieutenant Brheme,
Afliftant Engineer, Lieut. Davis of the royal
train of artillery, and two hundred Rangers)
about noon, in fifteen whale-boats; and that
night we encamped at la Chine; next morning we reached Ifle de Praires, and took a
view of the two Indian fettlements at Coyha-
vagu and Conefadagu.

On the 16th we got up to an ifland in the
Lake of St. Francis, and the next night encamped on the weftern fhore, at the lower end
of the upper rifts. We afcended thefe rifts
the day following, and continued all night
on the north-fhore, oppofite a number of iflands.

In the evening of the 19th we came to the
Ifle de Gallettes, and fpent the 20th in repair-
ing our whale-boats, which had received fome
damage in afcending the rifts.

D d   This

This morning I fent off ten fick Rangers to Albany, by the way of Ofwego, recommending them to the care of Col. Fitch, commanding at Ofwego, who was to give them fuitable directions.

We left Ifle de Gallettes on the 21ft; about twelve o'clock, the wind being unfavourable, we paffed Ofwegachi, and encamped but three miles above it on the northern fhore.

On the 22d we continued our courfe up the river, the wind blowing frefh at fouth, and halted in the evening at the narrow paffes near the iflands; but, upon the wind's abating at midnight, we embarked and rowed the remainder of that night, and the whole day following, till we came to the place where formerly ftood the old Fort of Frontiniac, where we found fome Indian hunters from Ofwegachi. We were detained here all the next day by the tempeftuoufnefs of the weather, which was very windy, attended with fnow and rain; we, however, improved the time in taking a plan of the old fort, fituated at the bottom of a fine fafe harbour.

There were about five hundred acres of cleared ground about it, which, tho' covered with clover, feemed bad and rocky, and interfperfed with fome pine-trees. The Indians
here

here feemed to be well pleafed with the news
we brought them of the furrender of all Canada, and fupplied us with great plenty of
venifon and wild fowl.

We left this place the 25th, about ten in the
morning, fteering a fouth-courfe two miles,
then weft fix miles, which brought us to the
mouth of a river thirty feet wide ; then fouth
four miles, where we halted to refrefh the
party.

About four in the afternoon we rowed for
a mountain bearing fouth-weft, which we did
not come up to till fome time in the night,
and found it to be a fteep rock, about one
hundred feet high. It now grew foggy, and
miftaking our way about fix miles, we rowed
all night, and till 8 o'clock next morning, before we put afhore ; which we then did on
a point, where we breakfafted, and then proceeded on our voyage, rowing till 8 o'clock at
night (being about one hundred miles, as we
imagined, from Frontiniac) we landed. This
evening we paffed two fmall iflands at the end
of a point extending far into the lake ; the
darknefs and fog prevented us from taking
fuch a furvey of them as to be able to give a
particular defcription of them.

The

The 27th of September, being very windy, we spent the time in deer-hunting, there being great plenty of them there, tho' the land is rocky, the timber bad, chiefly hemlock and pine; and I believe it is generally so on the north-side of Lake Ontario.

We embarked very early on the 28th, steering south-west, leaving a large bay on the right, about twenty miles wide; the western side of which terminates in a point, and a small island: having passed both, about fifteen miles on a course west by south, we entered the chops of a river, called by the Indians the *Grace of Man*; there we encamped, and found about 50 Mississagua Indians fishing for salmon. At our first appearance they ran down, both men and boys, to the edge of the lake, and continued firing their pieces, to express their joy at the sight of the English colours, till such time as we had landed.

They presented me with a deer just killed and split in halves, with the skin on, but the bowels taken out, which, with them, is a most elegant and polite present, and significant of the greatest respect. I told them of the success of their English brethren, against their fathers the French; at which they either were, or pretended to be, very well pleased.

Some

Some of us fished with them in the evening, being invited by them, and filled a bark-canoe with falmon in about half an hour. Their method of catching the fish is very extraordinary. One perfon holds a lighted pine-torch, while a fecond ftrikes the fish with a fpear. This is the feafon in which the falmon fpawn in thefe parts, contrary to what they do in any other place I ever knew them before.

I found the foil near this river very good and level. The timber is chiefly oak and maple, or the fugar-tree.

At feven o'clock the next morning we took our departure from this river, the wind being a-head. About fifteen miles further, on a weft-fouth-weft courfe, we put into another river, called the Life of Man. The Meffiffa-guas, who were hunting here, about thirty in number, paid us the fame compliments with thofe we juft before received from their coun-trymen, and, inftead of a deer, fplit up a young bear, and prefented me with it. Plenty of fifh was catched here alfo. The land conti-nued good and level, the foil of a blackish co-lour, and the banks of the lake were low.

The wind being fair the 30th, we embark-ed at the firft dawn of day, and with the af-fiftance of fails and oars, made great way on a

fouth-

south-west course, and in the evening reached the river Toronto, having run seventy miles. Many points extending far into the lake, occasioned a frequent alteration of our course. We passed a bank of twenty miles in length, but the land behind it seemed to be level, well-timbered with large oaks, hickaries, maples, and some poplars. No mountains appeared in sight. There was a track of about 300 acres of cleared ground, round the place where formerly the French had a fort, that was called Fort Toronto. The soil here is principally clay. The deer are extremely plenty in this country. Some Indians were hunting at the mouth of the river, who run into the woods at our approach, very much frightened. They came in, however, in the morning, and testified their joy at the news of our success against the French. They told us " that we could easily accomplish our journey from thence to Detroit in eight days: that when the French traded at that place, the Indians used to come with their poultry from Michlimakana, down the river Toronto: that the partage was but twenty miles from that to a river falling into Lake Huron, which had some falls, but none very considerable: they added, that there was a Carrying-place of fifteen miles
from

from some westerly part of Lake Erie, to a river running without any falls, thro' several Indian towns into Lake St. Clair.

I think Toronto a most convenient place for a factory, and that from thence we may very easily settle the north-side of Lake Erie.

We left Toronto the 1st of October, steering south, right across the west-end of Lake Ontario. At dark we arrived at the south-shore, five miles west of Fort Niagara, some of our boats being now become exceeding leaky and dangerous.

This morning, before we set out, I directed the following order of march:

" The boats in a line. If the wind rose high, the red flag hoisted, and the boats to crowd nearer, that they might be ready to give mutual assistance in case of a leak or other accident;" by which means we saved the crew and arms of the boat commanded by Lieut. M'Cormack, which sprung a leak and sunk, losing nothing except their packs.

We halted all the next day at Niagara, and provided ourselves with blankets, coats, shirts, shoes, magassins, &c.

I received from the commanding officer eighty barrels of provisions, and changed two whale-

whale-boats for as many battoes, which proved leaky.

In the evening some of my party proceeded with the provisions to the falls, and in the morning marched the rest there, and began the portage of the provisions and boats. Meff. Brheme and Davis took a survey of the great cataract of Niagara.

As the winter-season was now advancing very fast in this country, and I had orders to join Brig. Monkton from Presque Isle, wherever he might be, to receive his directions, I set out this evening, the 5th of October, in a bark-canoe, with Lieutenants Brheme and Holmes, and eight Rangers, leaving the command of my party to Capt. Brewer, with instructions to follow to Presque Isle, and encamped eight miles up the stream issuing out of Lake Erie. The land appeared to be good on both sides the river.

Next morning embarked early, and steered a south-west course. About noon opened Lake Erie, and leaving a bay to the left, we arrived by sun-set at the southern shore of the lake; we then steered west till eight o'clock at night, and drew up our boats on a sandy beach, forty miles distant from where we embarked in the morning.

The

The wind was very fresh next day, which prevented our setting out till 11 o'clock; so that we made no further progress than about twenty-eight miles on a west-south-west course. A little after noon, on the 8th of October, we arrived at Presque Isle, having kept a southerly course all the morning; I tarried there till 3 o'clock, when, having sent back my party to assist Capt. Brewer, Mr. Brheme, Lieutenant Holmes, and myself, took leave of Colonel Bouquet, who commanded at Presque Isle, and with three other men, in a bark-canoe, proceeded to French Creek, and at night encamped on the road, half way to Fort du Bouf. We got to this fort about 10 o'clock next day, and after three hours rest launched our canoe into the river, and paddled down about ten miles below the fort.

On the 10th we encamped at the second crossings of the river, the land on both sides appeared to be good all the way. The 11th we reached the Mingo Cabbins, and the night of the 12th we lodged at Venango; from thence went down the River Ohio; and on the morning of the 17th I waited upon Brigadier Monkton at Pittsburgh, and delivered him General Amherst's dispatches, and my own instructions.

I left

I left Pittſburgh the 20th, at the requeſt of General Monkton, who promiſed to ſend his orders after me to Preſque Iſle, by Mr. Croghan, and to forward Capt. Campbell immediately with a company of the Royal Americans; I got back to Preſque Iſle the 30th of October, Captain Campbell arrived the day after; Captain Brewer was got there before us, with the Rangers from Niagara, having loſt ſome of the boats, and part of the proviſions.

We immediately began to repair the damaged boats; and, as there was an account that a veſſel, expected with proviſions from Niagara, was loſt, I diſpatched Capt. Brewer by land to Detroit, with a drove of forty oxen, ſupplied by Col. Bouquet. Capt. Wait was about the ſame time ſent back to Niagara for more proviſions, and ordered to cruiſe along the north-coaſt of Lake Erie, and halt about twenty miles to the eaſt of the ſtreight between the Lakes Huron and Erie, till further orders. Brewer had a battoe to ferry his party over the Creeks, two horſes, and Capt. Monter with twenty Indians, compoſed of the Six Nations, Delawares and Shawaneſe, to protect him from the inſults of the enemy Indians.

My

My order of march over from Prefque Ifle was as follows:

"The boats to row two deep; firft, Major. Rogers's boat, abreaft of him Capt. Croghan; Capt. Campbell follows with his company, the Rangers next; and laftly, Lieutenant Holmes, who commands the rear-guard, with his own boat, and that of Enfign Wait's, fo as to be ready to affift any boat that may be in diftrefs. Boats in diftrefs are to fire a gun, when Mr. Holmes with the other boats under his command are immediately to go to their relief, take them to the fhore, or give fuch other affiftance as he thinks may be beft. When the wind blows hard, fo that the boats cannot keep their order, a red flag will be hoifted in the Major's boat; then the boats are not to mind their order, but put after the flag as faft as poffible to the place of landing, to which the flag-boat will always be a guide.

"It is recommended to the foldiers as well as officers, not to mind the waves of the lake; but when the furf is high to ftick to their oars, and the men at helm to keep the boat quartering on the waves, and brifkly follow, then no mifchief will happen by any ftorm whatever. Ten of the beft fteerfmen amongft the Rangers are to attend Captain Campbell and

company in his boats. It is likewife recommended to the officers commanding in thofe boats, to hearken to the fteerfmen in a ftorm or bad weather, in managing their boats. At evening, (if it is thought neceffary to row in the night-time) a blue flag will be hoifted in the Major's boat, which is the fignal for the boats to drefs, and then proceed in the following manner: the boats next the hindermoft, are to wait for the two in the rear, the two third boats for the fecond two; and fo on to the boats leading a-head, to prevent feparation, which in the night would be hazardous.

" Mr. Brheme is not to mind the order of march, but to fteer as is moft convenient for him to make his obfervations; he is however defired never to go more than a league a-head of the detachment, and is to join them at landing or encamping.

" On landing, the Regulars are to encamp in the center, and Lieutenant Holmes's divifion on the right wing with Mr. Croghan's people, Lieutenant M‘Cormick on the left wing with his divifion; Mr. Jequipe to be always ready with his Mohegan Indians, which are the picquet of the detachment, part of which are always to encamp in the front of the party; Capt. Campbell will mount a guard confifting

of

of one Subaltern, one Serjeant, and thirty privates, immediately on landing, for the security of his own encampment and battoes; Lieutenant Holmes's division to keep a guard of one Serjeant and ten Rangers on the right, and Lieutenant M'Cormick the like number on the left, and likewise to act as Adjutant to the detachment, and the orderly drum to attend him, to be at the Serjeant's call. The general to beat when ordered by the Major, at which time the whole party is to prepare for embarking, the troops half an hour after, when all the guards are to be called in, and the party embark immediately after.

" There is to be no firing of guns in this detachment without permission from the commanding officer, except when in distress on the lake. No man to go without the centries, when in camp, unless he has orders so to do; great care to be taken of the arms, and the officers to review them daily. Captain Campbell will order a drum to beat, for the regulation of his company when landed, at any time he thinks proper for parading his men, or reviewing their arms, &c.

" It is not doubted but due attention will be paid to all orders given.

" Mr.

" Mr. Croghan will, at landing, always attend the Major for orders, and to give such intelligence as he may have had from the Indians throughout the day."

We left Presque Isle the 4th of November, kept a western course, and by night had advanced twenty miles.

The badness of the weather obliged us to lie by all the next day; and as the wind continued very high, we did not advance more than ten or twelve miles the 6th, on a course west-south-west.

We set out very early on the 7th, and came to the mouth of Chogage River; here we met with a party of Attawawa Indians, just arrived from Detroit. We informed them of our success in the total reduction of Canada, and that we were going to bring off the French garrison at Detroit, who were included in the capitulation. I held out a belt, and told them I would take my brothers by the hand, and carry them to Detroit, to see the truth of what I had said. They retired, and held a council, and promised an answer next morning. That evening we smoaked the calamet, or pipe of peace, all the officers and Indians smoaking by turns out of the same pipe. The peace thus
con-

concluded, we went to reft, but kept good guards, a little diftrufting their fincerity.

The Indians gave their anfwer early in the morning, and faid their young warriors fhould go with me, while the old ones ftaid to hunt for their wives and children.

I gave them ammunition at their requeft, and a ftring of wampum in teftimony of my approbation, and charged them to fend fome of their fachems, or chiefs, with the party who drove the oxen along fhore; and they promifed to fpread the news, and prevent any annoyance from their hunters.

We were detained here by unfavourable weather till the 12th, during which time the Indians held a plentiful market in our camp of venifon and turkies.

From this place we fteered one mile weft, then a mile fouth, then four miles weft, then fouth-weft ten miles, then five miles weft-and-by-fouth, then fouth-weft eight miles, then weft-and-by-fouth feven miles, then four miles weft, and then fouth-weft fix miles, which brought us to Elk River, as the Indians call it, where we halted two days on account of bad weather and contrary winds.

On the 15th we embarked, and kept the following courfes; weft-fouth-weft two miles,

weft-

weft-north-weft three miles, weft-by-north one mile, weft two miles; here we paffed the mouth of a river, and then fteered weft one mile, weft-by-fouth two miles, weft-by-north four miles, north-weft three miles, weft-north-weft two miles, weft-by-north ten miles, where we encamped at the mouth of a river twenty-five yards wide.

The weather did not permit us to depart till the 18th, when our courfe was weft-by-fouth fix miles, weft-by-north four miles, weft two miles; here we found a river about fifteen yards over, then proceeded weft half a mile, weft-fouth-weft fix miles and a half, weft two miles and an half, north-weft two miles, where we encamped, and difcovered a river fixteen yards broad at the entrance.

We left this place the next day, fteering north-weft four miles, north-north-weft fix miles, which brought us to Sandufky Lake; we continued the fame courfe two miles, then north-north-eaft half a mile, north-weft a quarter of a mile, north the fame diftance, north-weft half a mile, north-by-eaft one furlong, north-weft-by-north one quarter of a mile, north-weft-by-weft one mile, weft-north-weft one mile, then weft half a mile, where we encamped near a fmall river, on the eaft-fide.

From

From this place I detached Mr. Brheme with a letter to Monfieur Beleter, the French commandant at Detroit, in thefe words:

To Capt. Beletere, *or the Officer commanding at Detroit.*

" SIR,

" That you may not be alarmed at the approach of the Englifh troops under my command, when they come to Detroit, I fend forward this by Lieut. Brheme, to acquaint you, that I have Gen. Amherft's orders to take poffeffion of Detroit, and fuch other pofts as are in that diftrict, which, by capitulation, agreed to and figned by the Marquis de Vaudreuil, and his Excellency Major Gen. Amherft, the 8th of September laft, now belong to the King of Great Britain.

" I have with me the Marquis de Vaudreuil's letters to you directed, for your guidance on this occafion, which letters I fhall deliver you when I arrive at or near your poft, and fhall encamp the troops I have with me at fome diftance from the fort, till you have reafonable time to be made acquainted with the Marquis de Vaudreuil's inftructions, and the

F f

capi-

capitulation, a copy of which I have with me likewife. I am,

SIR,

Your humble fervant,

Robert Rogers."

The land on the fouth-fide of Lake Erie, from Prefque Ifle, puts on a very fine appearance; the country level, the timber tall, and of the beft fort, fuch as oak, hickerie and locuft; and for game, both for plenty and variety, perhaps exceeded by no part of the world.

I followed Mr. Brheme on the 20th, and took a courfe north-weft four miles and an half, fouth-weft two, and weft three, to the mouth of a river in breadth 300 feet.

Here we found feveral Huron fachems, who told me, " that a body of 400 Indian warriors was collected at the entrance into the great ftreight, in order to obftruct our paffage; and that Monfieur Beleter had excited them to defend their country: that they were meffengers to know my bufinefs, and whether the

perfon

perſon I had ſent forward had reported the truth, that Canada was reduced " I confirmed this account, and that the fort at Detroit was given up by the French Governor. I preſented them a large belt, and ſpoke to this effect:

" Brothers,

" With this belt I take you by the hand. You are to go directly to your brothers aſſembled at the mouth of the river, and tell them to go to their towns till I arrive at the fort. I ſhall call you there as ſoon as Monſieur Beleter is ſent away, which ſhall be in two days after my arrival. We will then ſettle all matters. You live happily in your own country. Your brothers have long deſired to bring this about. Tell your warriors to mind their fathers (the French) no more, for they are all priſoners to your brothers (the Engliſh), who pitied them, and left them their houſes and goods, on their ſwearing by the Great One who made the world, to become as Engliſhmen forever. They are now your brothers; if you abuſe them, you affront me, unleſs they behave ill. Tell this to your brothers the Indians. What I ſay is truth. When we meet at Detroit I will convince you it is all true."

F f 2

Theſe

These sachems set out in good temper the next morning, being the 21st; but as the wind was very high, we did not move from this place.

On the 22d we encamped on a beach, after having steered that day north-west six miles, north-north-west four, to a river of the breadth of twenty yards, then north-west-by-west two miles, west-north-west one, west four, and west north-west five; it was with great difficulty we could procure any fuel here, the west-side of the Lake Erie abounding with swamps.

We rowed ten miles the next day, on a course north-west and by west, to Point Cedar, and then formed a camp; here we met some of the Indian messengers, to whom we had spoken two days before: they told us, their warriors were gone up to Monsieur Beleter, who, they said, is a strong man, and intends to fight you; a sachem of Attawawas was amongst them. All their Indians set out with us. The 24th we went north-west and by north ten miles, and fourteen miles north-east, to a long point; this night sixty of the Indian party came to our camp, who congratulated us on our arrival in their country, and offered themselves as an escort to Detroit, from whence they came the day before. They informed

formed me, that Mr. Bhreme and his party were confined; and that Monſieur Beleter had ſet up an high flag-ſtaff, with a wooden effigy of a man's head on the top, and upon that a crow; that the crow was to repreſent himſelf, the man's head mine, and the meaning of the whole, that he would ſcratch out my brains. This artifice, however, had no effect; for the Indians told him (as they ſaid) that the reverſe would be the true explanation of the ſign.

After we had proceeded ſix miles north-eaſt, we halted at the requeſt of the Indians, who deſired me to call in the chief Captains of the party at the Streight's mouth. I did ſo, and ſpent the 26th at the ſame place, in concilating their ſavage minds to peace and friendſhip.

The morning of the 27th, Monſieur Beleter ſent me the following letter by Monſieur Babee.

" Monsieur,

" J'ai reçu la lettre que vous m'avez écrite par un de vos Officiers; comme je n'ai point d'interprete, je ne puis faire la reponſe amplement.

L'Officier qui m'a remiſe la votre, me fait ſavoir qu'il étoit detaché afin de m'anoncer votre

votre arrivé, pour prendre poſſeſſion de cette
gariſon, ſelon la capitulation fait en Canada,
que vous avez conjointement avec un lettre de
Monſieur de Vaudreuil à mon addreſſe. Je
vous prie, Monſieur, d'arrêter vos troupes à
l'entrance de la riviere, juſques à ce que vous
m'envoyés la capitulation & la lettre de Mon-
ſeigneur le Marquis de Vaudreuil, afin de
pouvoir y conformer.

Je ſuis bien ſurpris qu'on ne m'a pas envoyé un Officier François avec vous, ſelon la
coûtume.

J'ai l'honneur d'étre, &c. &c.

De Beleter."

A Monſieur Monſieur *Rogers*,
   Major, & commandant le
   detachment Anglois."

In Engliſh thus.

" Sɪʀ,

" I received the letter you wrote me by one
of your Officers; but, as I have no interpreter,
cannot fully anſwer it.

The Officer that delivered me yours, gives
me to underſtand, that he was ſent to give me
                                          notice

notice of your arrival to take poſſeſſion of this garriſon, according to the capitulation made in Canada; that you have likewiſe a letter from Monſ. Vaudreuil directed to me. I beg, Sir, you'll halt your troops at the entrance of the river, till you ſend me the capitulation and the Marquis de Vaudreuil's letter, that I may act in conformity thereto.

I am ſurpriſed there is no French Officer ſent to me along with you, as is the cuſtom on ſuch occaſions. I have the honour to be, &c. &c.

De Beleter."

To Mr. *Rogers*, Major and
   Commander of the Eng-
   liſh detachment."

Shortly after a French party, under Captain Burrager, beat a parley on the weſt-ſhore; I ſent Mr. M'Cormick to know his buſineſs, who returned with the Officer and the following letter:

Detroit, le 25me Novembre, 1760.
" Monsieur,

" Je vous ai déja marqué par Monſieur Burrager les raiſons pourquoi je ne puis répon-
dre

dre en détail à la lettre qui m'a été remiſe le
22me du courant, par l'Officier que vous m'a-
vez detaché.

J'ignore les raiſons pourquoi il n'a pas vou-
lu retourner auprès de vous. J'ai envoyé mon
interprete Huron chez cette nation, que l'on
me dit être attroupé ſur le chemin de les con-
tenir, ne ſachant poſitivement ſi c'eſt à vous
ou à nous qu'ils en veuillent, & pour leur dire
de ma part, qu'ils ayent a ſe tenir tranquile-
ment ; que je ſavois ce que je devois à mon
General, & que de lorſque l'acte de la capitulation ſeroit reglé, j'étois obligé d'obéir. Le dit
interprete a ordre de vous attendre, & de vous
remettre la preſent. Ne ſoyez point ſurpris,
Monſieur, ſi ſur le long de la côte vous trouve-
rez nos habitans ſur leur garde ; on leur a an-
noncé qu'il y avoit beaucoup de nations à votre
ſuite, à qui on avois promis le pillage, & que
leſdites nations étoient même determinées à
vous le demander ; je leur ai permis de regar-
der, c'eſt pour vôtre conſervation & ſureté ainſi
que pour la nôtre, en cas que les dites nations
devenoient à faire les inſolents, vous ſeul ne ſe-
riez peut-être pas dans les circonſtances pre-
ſentes en état de les reduire. Je me flatte, Monſieur, que ſi tôt que la preſent vour ſera par-
venue, vous voudriez bien m'envoyer par quel-
qu'un

qu'un de vos Meſſieurs, & la capitulation & la lettre de Monſieur Vaudreuil. J'ai l'honneur d'être,

MONSIEUR,

Votre tres-humble & obéiſſant ſerviteur,

Pign. de Beletere."

A Monſieur Monſieur *Rogers*,
Major, commandant le de-
tachment Anglois au bas de
la riviere.

In Engliſh thus :

" SIR, Detroit, 25th Nov. 1760.

" I have already by Mr. Barrager acquainted you with the reaſons why I could not anſwer particularly the letter which was delivered me the 22d inſtant by the Officer you ſent
to me.

" I am entirely unacquainted with the reaſons of his not returning to you. I ſent my
Huron interpreter to that nation, and told him
to ſtop them, ſhould they be on the road, not
knowing poſitively whether they were inclined

G g to

to favour you or us, and to tell them from me they fhould behave peaceably; that I knew what I owed to my General, and that when the capitulation fhould be fettled I was obliged to obey. The faid interpreter has orders to wait on you, and deliver you this.

" Be not furprifed, Sir, if along the coaft you find the inhabitants upon their guard; it was told them you had feveral Indian nations with you, to whom you had promifed permiffion to plunder, nay, that they were even refolved to force you to it. I have therefore allowed the faid inhabitants to take to their arms, as it is for your fafety and prefervation as well as ours; for fhould thefe Indians become infolent, you may not perhaps, in your prefent fituation, be able to fubdue them alone.

" I flatter myfelf, Sir, that, as foon as that fhall come to hand, you will fend me by fome of the Gentlemen you have with you, both the capitulation and Monfieur Vaudreuil's letter. I have the honour to be,

   Sir,

     Your very humble and obedient fervant,

To Major Rogers.

       Pign. Beletere."

We

We encamped the next day five miles up the river, having rowed againſt the wind; and on the 29th I diſpatched Captain Campbell, with Meſſieurs Barrager and Babee, and their parties, with this letter.

" Sir,

" I acknowledge the receipt of your two letters, both of which were delivered to me yeſterday. Mr. Erheme has not yet returned. The incloſed letter from the Marquis de Vaudreuil will inform you of the ſurrender of all Canada to the King of Great Britain, and of the great indulgence granted to the inhabitants; as alſo of the terms granted to the troops of his Moſt Chriſtian Majeſty. Captain Campbell, whom I have ſent forward with this letter, will ſhew you the capitulation. I deſire you will not detain him, as I am determined, agreeable to my inſtructions from General Amherſt, ſpeedily to relieve your poſt. I ſhall ſtop the troops I have with me at the hither end of the town till four o'clock, by which time I expect your anſwer; your inhabitants under arms will not ſurpriſe me, as yet I have ſeen no other in that poſition, but ſavages waiting for my orders. I can aſſure you, Sir, the

G g 2   in-

inhabitants of Detroit fhall not be molefted, they and you complying with the capitulation, but be protected in the quiet and peaceable poffeffion of their eftates ; neither fhall they be pillaged by my Indians, nor by your's that have joined me.

I am, &c.

To Capt. Beletere,   *R. Rogers.*"
commanding at Detroit.

I landed at half a mile fhort of the fort, and fronting it, where I drew up my detachment on a field of grafs. Here Capt. Campbell joined me, and with him came a French officer, to inform me that he bore Monfieur Beletere's compliments, fignifying he was under my command. From hence I fent Lieutenants Leflie and M'Cormack, with thirty-fix Royal Americans, to take poffeffion of the fort. The French garrifon laid down their arms, Englifh colours were hoifted, and the French taken down, at which about 700 Indians gave a fhout, merrily exulting in their prediction being verified, that the crow reprefented the Englifh.

They

They feemed amazed at the fubmiffive fa-
lutations of the inhabitants, expreffed their fatisfaction at our generofity in not putting them
to death, and faid they would always for the
future fight for a nation thus favoured by Him
that made the world.

I went into the fort, received a plan of it,
with a lift of the ftores, from the commanding
officer, and by noon of the 1ft of December
we had collected the militia, difarmed them,
and to them alfo adminiftered the oaths of allegiance.

The interval from this time to the 9th was
fpent in preparing to execute fome meafures
that appeared to be neceffary to the fervice we
were upon. I put Monfieur Beletere and the
other prifoners under the care of Lieut. Holmes
and thirty Rangers, to be carried to Philadelphia; and ordered Capt. Campbell and his
company to keep poffeffion of the fort. Lieut.
Butler and Enfign Wait were fent with a detached party of twenty men, to bring the
French troops from the forts Miamie and Ga-
tanois. I ordered, that, if poffible, a party
fhould fubfift at the former this winter, and
give the earlieft notice at Detroit of the enemy's motions in the country of the Illinois.
I fent Mr. M'Gee, with a French officer, for
the

the French troops at the Shawanese town on the Ohio. And as provisions were scarce, directed Capt. Brewer to repair with the greatest part of the Rangers to Niagara, detaining Lieut. M'Cormack with thirty-seven more, to go with me to Michlimakana.

I made a treaty with the several tribes of Indians living in the neighbouring country; and having directed Capt. Wait, just arrived from Niagara, to return again thither immediately, I set out for Lake Huron, and on the night of the 10th encamped at the north-end of the little Lake St. Clair, and the next even-on the west-side of the streight, at the entrance of a considerable river, where many Indians were hunting. We opened Lake Huron the day following, and saw many Indian hunters on both sides of the mouth of the streights. We coasted along the west-shore of the Lake, about twenty miles north-and-by-west, the next day being the 13th forty, and the 15th thirty-eight miles, passing the cakes of ice with much difficulty. We could not advance all the 16th, a heavy north-wind setting the cakes of ice on the south-shore in such quantities, that we could find no passage between them. I consulted the Indians about a journey to Michlimakana across by land; but
they

they declared it impracticable at this feafon without fnow-fhoes, and to our great mortification we were obliged to return to Detroit; the ice obftructing us fo much, that, with the greateft diligence and fatigue, we did not arrive there till the 21ft.

I delivered the ammunition to Capt. Campbell, and on the 23d fet out for Pittfburg, marching along the weft-end of Lake Erie, till the 2d of January 1761, when we arrived at Lake Sandufky.

I have a very good opinion of the foil from Detroit to this place; it is timbered principally with white and black oaks, hickerie, locufts, and maple. We found wild apples along the weft end of Lake Erie, fome rich favannahs of feveral miles extent, without a tree, but cloathed with jointed grafs near fix feet high, which, rotting there every year, adds to the fertility of the foil, The length of Sandufky is about fifteen miles from eaft to weft, and about fix miles acrofs it. We came to a town of the Windot Indians, where we halted to refrefh.

On January 3d, fouth-eaft-by-eaft three miles, eaft-by-fouth one mile and a half, fouth-eaft a mile through a meadow, croffed a fmall creek about fix yards wide, running
eaft,

eaft, travelled fouth-eaft-by-eaft one mile, paffed thro' Indian houfes, fouth-eaft three quarters
of a mile, and came to a fmall Indian town of
about ten houfes.   There is a remarkable fine
fpring at this place, rifing out of the fide
of a fmall hill with fuch force, that it boils
above the ground in a column three feet high.
I imagine it difcharges ten hogfheads of water
in a minute.   From this town our courfe was
fouth-fouth-eaft three miles, fouth two miles,
croffed a brook about five yards wide, running
eaft-fouth-eaft, travelled fouth one mile, croffed a brook about four yards wide, running
eaft-fouth-eaft, travelled fouth-fouth-eaft two
miles, croffed a brook about eight yards wide.
This day we killed plenty of deer and turkies
on our march, and encamped.

On the 4th we travelled fouth-fouth-eaft
one mile, and came to a river about twenty-five
yards wide, croffed the river, where are two
Indian houfes, from thence fouth-by-eaft one
mile, fouth-fouth-eaft one mile and a half,
fouth-eaft two miles, fouth-fouth-eaft one mile,
and came to an Indian houfe, where there was
a family of Windots hunting, from thence
fouth-by-eaft a quarter of a mile, fouth five
miles, came to the river we croffed this morning; the courfe of the river here is weft-
north-

north-weſt. This day killed ſeveral deer and other game, and encamped.

On the 5th travelled ſouth-ſouth-weſt half a mile, ſouth one mile, ſouth-ſouth-weſt three quarters of a mile, ſouth half a mile, croſſed two ſmall brooks running eaſt, went a ſouth-ſouth-weſt courſe half a mile, ſouth half a mile, ſouth-eaſt half a mile, ſouth two miles, ſouth-eaſt one mile, ſouth half a mile, croſſed a brook running eaſt-by-north, travelled ſouth-by-eaſt half a mile, ſouth ſouth-eaſt two miles, ſouth-eaſt three quarters of a mile, ſouth-ſouth-eaſt one mile, and came to Maſkongom Creek, about eight yards wide, croſſed the creek, and encamped about thirty yards from it. This day killed deer and turkies in our march.

On the 6th we travelled about fourteen or fifteen miles, our general courſe being about eaſt-ſouth-eaſt, killed plenty of game, and encamped by a very fine ſpring.

The 7th our general courſe about ſouth-eaſt, travelled about ſix miles, and croſſed Maſkongom Creek, running ſouth, about twenty yards wide. There is an Indian town about twenty yards from the creek, on the eaſt-ſide, which is called the Mingo Cabbins. There were but two or three Indians in the place, the reſt were

H h   hunting.

hunting. Thefe Indians have plenty of cows, horfes, hogs, &c.

The 8th, halted at this town to mend our mogafons, and kill deer, the provifions I brought from Detroit being entirely expended. I went a-hunting with ten of the Rangers, and by ten o'clock got more venifon than we had occafion for.

On the 9th travelled about twelve miles, our general courfe being about fouth-eaft, and encamped by the fide of a long meadow, where there were a number of Indians hunting.

The 10th, about the fame courfe, we travelled eleven miles, and encamped, having killed in our march this day three bears and two elks.

The 11th, continuing near the fame courfe, we travelled thirteen miles and encamped, where were a number of Wiandots and Six Nation Indians hunting.

The 12th, travelled fix miles, bearing rather more to the eaft, and encamped. This evening we killed feveral beaver.

The 13th, travelled about north-eaft fix miles, and came to the Delaware's town, called Beaver Town. This Indian town ftands on good land, on the weft-fide of the Maf-kongom

kongom River; and oppofite to the town, on the eaft-fide, is a fine river, which difcharges itfelf into it. The latter is about thirty yards wide, and the Mafkongom about forty; fo that when they both join, they make a very fine ftream, with a fwift current, running to the fouth-weft. There are about 3000 acres of cleared ground round this place. The number of warriors in this town is about 180. All the way from the Lake Sandufky I found level land, and a good country. No pine-trees of any fort; the timber is white, black, and yellow oak, black and white walnut, cyprus, chefnut, and locuft trees. At this town I ftaid till the 16th in the morning to refrefh my party, and procured fome corn of the Indians to boil with our venifon.

On the 16th we marched nearly an eaft courfe about nine miles, and encamped by the fide of a fmall river.

On the 17th kept much the fame courfe, croffing feveral rivulets and creeks. We travelled about twenty miles, and encamped by the fide of a fmall river.

On the 18th we travelled about fixteen miles an eafterly courfe, and encamped by a brook.

The 19th, about the fame general courfe, we croffed two confiderable ftreams of water,

H h 2   and

and some large hills timbered with chefnut and oak, and having travelled about twenty miles, we encamped by the fide of a fmall river, at which place were a number of Delawares hunting.

On the 20th, keeping ftill an eafterly courfe, and having much the fame travelling as the day before, we advanced on our journey about nineteen miles, which brought us to Beaver Creek, where are two or three Indian houfes, on the weft fide of the creek, and in fight of the Ohio.

Bad weather prevented our journeying on the 21ft, but the next day we profecuted our march. Having croffed the creek, we travelled twenty miles, nearly fouth-eaft, and encamped with a party of Indian hunters.

On the 23d we came again to the Ohio, oppofite to Fort Pitt, from whence I ordered Lieut. M'Cormack to march the party acrofs the country to Albany, and, after tarrying there till the 26th, I came the common road to Philadelphia, from thence to New York, where, after this long, fatiguing tour, I arrived February 14, 1761.

F I N I S.

ADVERTISEMENT.

IT is propofed to continue this JOURNAL, in a fecond volume, containing an account of my travels into the country of the Cherokees, and the fouthern Indians; of my fecond tour into the interior country, upon the great lakes; and of the Indian wars in America fince the year 1760; together with correct plans of all the Britifh forts upon the continent. To be publifhed by fubfcription.

Subfcriptions are taken in by JOHN MILLAN, Bookfeller, near Whitehall, and by fuch others as he fhall appoint, he being impowered by me for that purpofe, and will give proper receipts to deliver the faid volume, or return the fubfcription-money, within a limited time.

The price to fubfcribers will be one Englifh Guinea; one half to be paid at fubfcribing, and the other on the delivery of the book.

BOOKS Printed for J. MILLAN, near Whitehall.

1. REgimental and Recruiting Books, with proper Heads, engraved.

2. Pettiver's Syftem of Natural Hiftory, with feveral Thoufand Figures on 300 large Folio Copper Plates, 100 of which never before publifhed, 6l. 6s.

3. Dillenius's General Hiftory of Land and Water Moffes, Corals, &c. about 1000 Figures on 85 Royal Quarto Copper Plates, drawn and finely engraved by the Author, 1l. 5s.

4. Sheldrake's Herbal, on above 100 large Folio Copper Plates, drawn in the moft mafterly Manner from the Originals when in their higheft Perfeꞙion.

5. Sheldrake on Heat and Cold for Green Houfes, 1s.

6. Columella on Agriculture, by Gibfon, 14s.

7. Palladio finely engraved by Ware, 7s. 6d.

8. Hill's Hiftory of the Royal Society, 10s. 6d.

9. Dr. Sharpe's Englifh, Hebrew, and Englifh Latin Grammars.

10. Dr.Sharpe'sDefence of Chriftianity, 3s. Oligarchy, 1s.

11. Letters from a Perfian in England, 3s.

12. Langley's Gothic Architeꞙure, 15s.

13. ——— Treafury of Defigns, 15s.

14. ——— Builder's Jewel, 6s.

15. Inigo Jones's Defigns for Chimnies, Ceilings, Temples, &c. 10s. 6d.

16. Pine's Horace, 2 vols. 2l. 2s.

17. Muller's Syftem of Mathematicks, Fortification, Artillery, Engineering, &c. with large Additions, and 130 Cuts. 7 vol. in 6. 2l. 6s. or any volume feperate.

18. A Syftem of Camp Difcipline, Adjutant's Duty, Garrifon Duty, Regulations for the Land Forces, Kane's Campaigns and Military Hiftory, from 1660, with many Copper Plates, 7s. 6d. in the Prefs.

19. New Pruffian Field Regulations for Foot, with 19 large fine Plates, 7s. 6d.

20. Returns Weekly, Monthly, and General Atteftations, Furloughs, Difcharges, &c.

21. Lift

BOOKS Printed for J. MILLAN, near Whitehall.

21. Lift of the Army at Home and Abroad.

22. Tandon's French Grammar, to learn without a Mafter, 5th Edition, 2s.

23. Morris's Lectures on Architecture, 2 Parts, 6s.

24. Capt. Miller's Art of Self-Defence, 10s. 6d.

25. Capt. Bontien's large Map of Jamaica, corrected to 1765. 7s. 6d.

26. Drummer's Inftructor, with the Englifh and Scotch Duty, Beatings, Marches, Calls, &c. neatly engraved, on 12 Plates, by R. Spencer, Serjeant Major in the Foot Guards, 1s.

27. Prior's Pofthumous Works, 2 vols. 8vo. 10s.

28. Buckingham's Works, 2 vols. 8vo.

29. Price's Carpentry, 4to.

30. Pocock's Theological Works, 2 vols. folio.

The following compiled by J. MILLAN.

31. Signals and Flags of all Nations, 5s.

32. Coins, Weights, and Meafures of all Nations, Antient and Modern, 5s.

33. Succeffion of Colonels to each Regiment to 1765.

34. Peerage of Great-Britain and Ireland, to 1765, 15s.

35. Baronetage of England, 5s.

36. Complete Card-Player, 2s.

37. Univerfal Regifter of Court and City Offices, the only complete of the Kind, 2s. 6d. or 3s. with an Almanack.

38. Lifts of the Forces of above 40 Sovereigns, &c. Ranks, Uniforms, Number of Officers, Private Men, &c. Neatly coloured, 10s. 6d.

DATE DUE
